The School Play

A COMPLETE HANDBOOK

The School Play
A COMPLETE HANDBOOK

Peter Griffith

Batsford Academic and Educational Limited London

© Peter Griffith 1981

ISBN 0 7134 3541 0

First published in Great Britain 1981

Phototypesetting by Typewise Limited, Wembley
Printed in Great Britain by
Billing & Son Ltd., London Guildford & Worcester
for the publishers
Batsford Academic and Educational Limited
an imprint of B T Batsford Ltd
4 Fitzhardinge Street
London W1H 0AH

Contents

About the book

Putting on the School Play can be a daunting task for the teacher in charge of the project. It can also be the source of creative achievement and educational value for everyone – teachers and pupils – involved in the production. This practical guide takes the would-be producer through every step of the process, beginning with the reasons for doing it, choosing the play; planning the production; casting; rehearsals; backstage, including props, costumes, scenery, dress rehearsals, lighting, make-up, sound and stage management; publicity; finance; dress rehearsal and performance.

The appendices include a glossary of theatrical jargon, a 'potted' 12-week production schedule, a selective bibliography and a list of plays suitable for production in a school.

Peter Griffith's experience and obvious love of the theatre have enabled him to write in an entertaining and down-to-earth way about all sorts of problems and pitfalls unimagined by the newcomer. He also provides a host of practical suggestions which will help the producer, his cast and everyone involved in the production to survive until the first night *and* make the play a success. To read this book is to want to take part in such a production.

About the Author

Peter Griffith was born in Tunbridge Wells and educated at Cranleigh School and Durham University, where he gained a degree in English. He trained as a teacher of Drama, English and Music at Leeds University, and he also gained a Licentiateship of Guildhall School of Music and Drama. While at university he acted in and directed numerous plays, and sang lead roles in several operas. For five years he was Head of Drama at Sandown Court School, Tunbridge Wells, during which time he produced a total of 22 plays – including a multi-school **West Side Story,** and the British amateur premiere of **Grease** (in the days before anyone had heard of John Travolta). During his free moments at this time he wrote plays and music, sang semi-professionally, conducted a local choir, and acted in many more plays; then in 1978 he left teaching to become a full-time actor, and founded the White Horse Travelling Theatre – a small professional theatre company based in Wells, Somerset, which operates in schools throughout Southern England, and performs in village halls, barns, fields, streets, and theatres mainly in the Mendip region. The company also makes occasional visits to Northern England and to the continent; and it allows Mr Griffith scope to exercise his multifarious interests in acting, writing plays, directing, drinking, composing, singing, playing instruments – and writing books about how to produce The School Play.

Preface

This book is the fruit of five years' experience teaching drama and producing school plays (a total of 22 productions) in a secondary modern school in Kent. Neither the productions nor the book would have been possible were it not for the enthusiasm – and co-operation way beyond the call of duty – of all my former colleagues at Sandown Court School; and it is important that I should stress that the various characters who feature among these pages – the Headmaster, the Head of Physical Education, the school caretaker, etc – are in no way intended as portraits of actual people with whom I worked during my years in Tunbridge Wells, but rather as hypothetical figures whom the reader might care to identify with any characters in his own school.

My thanks are due to Dave Hollis, Ruth Moore and Simon Persighetti for ploughing through the first draft of the book and giving me their most valuable comments; to John Coultas for his help with Appendix IV; to Gertrude Sofrin for her assistance with preparation of the manuscript; and to my partners in White Horse Travelling Theatre for humouring my insomniac irritability as the publisher's deadline approached.

I hope that the book will be of practical assistance to those about to embark upon their first production; and that it will be of moral assistance to hardened producers who may find it reassuring to know that they are not the only ones who face problems when they attempt to produce The School Play.

1 Why put on a play?

So you want to produce a school play? Let's be under no illusions. You are letting yourself in for some twelve weeks of fatigue, frustration and overwork. However well organized you may be for the first eight of those twelve weeks, in the last four of them you are going to be shattered and exhausted as the monster you have created drags you through crisis after crisis towards the opening night, taking up every moment of your spare time plus a lot of time that you can't spare. You will get little sympathy from your colleagues, most of whom will be quite unaware of the amount of work involved in theatre, and will regard the play as an unwelcome and trivial disruption of their comfortable routine; you will get little sympathy from your pupils, who regard you as superhuman and infallible and blame you for everything; and you may get little sympathy from your Headmaster, who will probably regard the whole exercise as a conspiracy to spend the school fund money behind his back, and will guffaw jovially when you suggest naively that you ought to be paid extra for the amount of time you are devoting to the production, and then ask you why you are so late with your reports.

Do you still want to produce a school play? If I've put you off already, you may as well return this book to the shelf where you found it.

If you are undeterred, then we can begin to look on the positive side. If all goes well, you are letting yourself in for twelve weeks of creative endeavour and artistic achievement that will remain with some of your pupils for the rest of their lives as the most enjoyable, most valuable and most memorable weeks of their entire schooldays.

Once you have established in your own mind that you are going ahead with a production, your first task is to convince your pupils, your colleagues and your head teacher that you are serious, and that the production will be of benefit to them all. To this end, before even choosing the play, you need to be clear in your own mind – and lucid in convincing others – as to the reasons for having a school play at all. What are the educational benefits that can justify the vast expense of time and effort that will be involved? And is the gargantuan exercise principally for the benefit of the school's best actors, or the school community as a whole, or the Headmaster's desire to impress the governors and the local press?

Clearly this is a leading question. My answer – and the premise upon which much of this book is based – is that at its best the school play is a project that involves in some way every member of the school community (staff as well as pupils) in a joint endeavour, unifying the school in a collective responsibility. Naturally the greatest benefit will be felt by the cast: but this should not consist merely of a handful of the school's best actors. Ideally there should be the opportunity for every pupil who is willing to commit himself to the project to appear on stage. Your cast will have the chance to learn something of acting technique and to develop self-confidence and self-discipline. And furthermore they will discover the vital truth that acting does not depend on individual talent and 'star quality' (as the media would have us believe) but on total teamwork and group awareness: and through this they will – if all goes well – experience the euphoria of an artistically successful production.

But as well as all this, it is important that there should be the opportunity for pupils at all levels of the school to be involved in building and painting scenery, designing and sewing costumes, finding and making props, designing and printing posters, and all the other areas of work that go on behind the scenes of a major theatrical production. Beyond this, every child and every member of staff should be involved in publicizing the performances – putting up posters and actively selling tickets. And furthermore, as many departments of the school as possible should use the theme or period of the play, or activities connected with the production, as a focus for their syllabuses during the term in question. By the time of the first performance, every single child should feel that he has contributed in some way, even if it is only by making a sword in a woodwork lesson, drawing a picture for display in the foyer, or persuading the local grocer to exhibit a poster.

In other words, the play is a project involving the entire school: and what is more, if successful it will not only cover its costs financially, but it will also be a splendid public relations exercise for the school, in which the general public will see artistic work of a high standard being produced, and through the mass involvement of the pupils both the morale and the public image of the school will be raised. At its best, the School Play has the effect of strengthening the whole fabric of the school community. To explain in practical terms how to set about producing a play along these idealistic lines is one of the purposes of this book.

The other main purpose of the book concerns you, the play's director – the harrassed spider at the hub of the vast web I have just described. You are the instigator of the whole project – to risk another metaphor, the flung stone that sets ripples spreading out across the entire width of the school (at, to pursue the metaphor to its conclusion, the imminent risk of your own drowning). And it is of vital importance that you know what you are doing.

Figure 1

So many children who have never visited a theatre have an inbuilt idea that theatre is dry and boring, and it would be a major tragedy if a badly-directed school play were to confirm this view in any of them. No-one expects top-quality acting from children (though it can be achieved where drama is a part of the curriculum right through the school), but there is no reason why the directing of the play – the grouping, the timing, and the inventiveness of the production ideas – should be at anything less than the highest standards of professional theatre. Nor is there any reason why young actors, already terrified by the trauma of being on stage in front of their friends, should be hampered by amateurish lighting, bungled scene-changes, and collapsible props. As the play's director you are the expert – if you are unlucky, the only expert in the school

13

– to whom everyone will turn. In a school situation it is inevitable that many things will be beyond your control; but there is no excuse for allowing any part of your own contribution to the project – the artistic credibility of the production, and its technical and administrative smoothness – to be in any way weak, shoddy, or 'amateurish'. The worst conceivable condemnation of your production is the oft-heard patronising comment: 'Well it was very good…considering it was a school play.'

My intention is that this book can be a reference manual which will explain in simple practical terms the business of directing and producing a play, and – a separate but related topic – the business of doing so in a school environment.

And now to choose your play.

2 Choosing a play: the criteria

Your choice of a play involves a number of conflicting criteria. It is impossible to achieve the highest possible artistic standard as well as involving the maximum number of pupils, and so whatever you choose as your main school play must represent a compromise between these two extremes.

Of course, a school with a thriving drama department will want to put on many more than one play per year. It is good to be able, in different small-scale productions, to give experienced actors the chance to try 'meaty' parts; to give drama specialist classes the chance to work on experimental theatre; to give GCE literature classes the chance to gain practical experience of the plays they are studying; to give groups at all levels of the school the chance to inprovise their own plays; to give dancers and singers the chance to shine; and to give children the chance to involve themselves in the local community by taking drama out of school. But the function of the School Play (with capital S and P) remains, separate from all these issues, to unify the whole school, if possible, in a piece of extended work that is stimulating for the cast, the backstage crew, the children and the adult audience alike. It must be on this basis that your play is chosen.

The conflict still remains. You want the play:

(a) to be 'good drama'
(b) to stretch the ability of your best actors
(c) to contain parts for everybody who is enthusiastic
(d) to be entertaining and/or educational for the children in the audience
(e) to be entertaining and/or prestigious and impressive for the adults in the audience.

I have yet to discover the play that will satisfy all these aims: so each criterion must be considered and evaluated.

(a) That it should be 'good drama'

To choose a play by an established author – possibly even one which features on the English Literature syllabus – may have a number of advantages. You will have little difficulty in convincing your Head Teacher, your colleagues and the academic world at large of the educational desirability of acquainting your pupils with Shakespeare, Shaw, or any of the great playwrights. What is more, the English department may already have the copies in stock, and if the dramatist in question has been dead more than 50 years there are no royalties to be paid – both good money-saving facts that will appeal to the Headmaster.

Your problems start, however, when you try to sell the literary masterpiece to your pupils. To maintain the enthusiasm of large numbers of children a play needs to be immediate, vigorous, and preferably strongly visual with plenty of movement. Most 'great drama' has a major verbal content. It is great literature: and to perform it effectively needs a high degree of Thespian artistry – in particular, a strong and well modulated voice with plenty of controlled variation, and the experience and maturity to convey the subtleties of character and situation through nuances of timing and gesture. While it is not impossible to achieve these qualities in children, it is extremely difficult; my advice is that it is best done – initially at least – with a small group of pupils (say perhaps a Drama 'O' Level group) rather than attempted with a large mixed-ability cast.

The impact upon the audience needs to be considered as well. The danger is that, unless you are working with an exceptionally gifted group of pupils, you may discourage the children in your audience from an appreciation of great drama by failing to convey the dramatic situations behind the words. The language of our great authors is generally literary and in some cases old-fashioned: unless you are fully confident that you can get your cast to understand and communicate the drama behind that language, then your production will be no more than a costumed recitation, and you will have done a grave disservice to cast and audience alike, as well as having risked causing a dignified and respected playwright to turn in his Westminster Abbey tomb.

However, there is another way of interpreting the phrase 'good drama'. It is essential that you choose a play with a theme that is both accessible and relevant to your pupils. It needs to involve conflicts and situations which your cast will understand and identify with. Even if it is not by an author one thinks of as 'great' it needs to have artistic integrity and a plot the unfolding of which will stimulate and illuminate the lives of cast and audience alike. It can – and should – be 'good drama' regardless of whether or not it is great literature. At the basis of your choice must rest the fact that the play is to be performed and appreciated by children, and it must be drama that is 'good' by being appropriate for the age-range and experience of your pupils.

(b) That it should stretch the ability of your best actors

Within every school there are some children with obvious dramatic talent and/or exceptional enthusiasm, who will want to be involved in whatever drama is going on, and will badger you for the best parts. There may even be a few pupils who are seriously contemplating a career in the theatre, and will be wanting to gain experience of major roles to help them in auditioning for drama colleges. Naturally you wish to do the best you can to stretch the ability and foster the enthusiasm of these pupils, and so the ideal play will contain a reasonable number of challenging roles for your most experienced actors.

It is best to avoid a play that depends heavily on one or two main characters: a part involving vast amounts of learning and an intense emotional commitment can put too much of a burden onto a pupil who is trying at the same time to cope with homework and growing up. And more important, a reliance on the talents of one or two main actors can create an invidious feeling of 'stars' and ferment jealousy within the cast and conceit in the principal performers. It is far preferable to find a play that offers at least ten fairly equal main roles, so as to promote the spirit of interdependance among your actors which is the ideal of a good production.

For reasons which I cannot fully explain, it is often the case that your best actors will include a number of pupils who find it difficult to adjust to school discipline and are the bane of other members of staff. Involvement in drama can often be of exceptional benefit to these pupils; but it is vital that their involvement is such as to promote self-discipline, responsibility and group identity, rather than encouraging bigheadedness in a pupil who already likes to think of himself as a star and disrupts other teachers' lessons in an effort to prove this. So your ideal play must be selected on the basis of its being an educational experience, and not merely an ego-trip, for your principal actors: and to this end it needs to have a reasonable spread of main roles, with none being unduly predominant.

(c) That there should be parts for everyone who is enthusiastic

Provided that they are willing to commit themselves to the production, those children who arguably stand to gain most from the School Play are the great mass of those who lack the ability or confidence to handle a major role, but who can gain both ability and confidence through appearing on stage in a small or non-speaking or chorus role. Here again you will need to reach a compromise between the artistic and educational requirements of the project. The most artistically satisfying production you could mount would probably have a cast of no more than six pupils; but that is not the aim of a School Play. So you need to choose something that gives opportunities for onstage and offstage participation to large numbers of pupils to the level of each child's ability.

A child who is uncoordinated and unconfident can develop almost visibly from rehearsal to rehearsal, provided that he is not asked to do something that will expose him to the ridicule of others. But the same child, if consistently rejected because he is 'not good enough', will inevitably become even less confident and possibly more resentful. The purpose of the School Play is not to create young stars, but to give as many pupils as possible, at all levels of ability, the chance to collaborate creatively and develop through this collaboration: your choice of play must always bear this in mind.

(d) That it should be entertaining and/or educational for children in the audience

If you wish the whole school to want to be involved in your production and your cast to feel that the show was a success, then the eventual performance must be found enjoyable and entertaining by the children in the audience. This doesn't necessarily mean that it has to be a comedy or a farce; but it means it must never be boring, and it must appeal to the age-range of the children in your school.

To fulfil this criterion, you may well be tempted to put on a play which is, frankly, trivial. This doesn't necessarily matter, provided that the material is not actually anti-educational (eg encouraging a flippant or unduly cynical approach to morality), because you may well decide – based upon your assessment of the children involved – that the project as a whole requires a play that is more entertaining than educative. Of course these two factors are not mutually exclusive, and you may come up with a play that will effectively

18

educate its audience without losing entertainment value. But if you can teach the children in your school that theatre is alive and exciting, by means of a trivial play that is well done and entertaining, that will probably have more educational value than a more 'meaty' or a more didactic play performed with less conviction and less audience enthusiasm.

(e) That it is prestigious and impressive for the adults in the audience

You may not initially feel all that strongly about whether the play will enhance the reputation of the school in the local community; but the Headmaster, who has to carry the can as far as the parents and the general public are concerned, will impress the point on you in no uncertain terms.

It cannot be denied that the image of the school in the eyes of the local press and the general public can make a considerable difference to the way pupils feel about their school, and consequently to the atmosphere within the school. The school play is one of the few events in the year when the school puts itself on show to parents and the public, and this makes it important that the play should create a favourable impression among the adults in the audience. It is to be hoped that this consideration will not force you to compromise on the artistic and educational content of the project. If you feel that the play you have chosen will not be appreciated by some of the more staid adults who see it, then with luck, a brief programme note explaining the purpose of The School Play (you may quote from Chapter One of this book if you wish) will put matters to rights. But it is a criterion that needs to be born in mind, and a line of attack against which you may have to defend your choice of play.

It may even prove necessary – astonishingly in this day and age – to defend your right to produce a play involving members of the lower social orders. I have on several occasions received complaints from parents and senior staff who are unaware of the distinction between elocution and drama that I have 'failed to correct' the local accents of some of my cast who were appearing on stage as robbers or pirates. Once again your task is to stick by your assessment of what is best for your pupils, and try gently to educate the public as to what School Plays are for. It is bad enough that a whole section of your pupils are likely to begin with the opinion that 'all actors are poofs' without senior teachers and citizens unwittingly confirming this opinion by trying to impose 'correct' elocution onto all theatre regardless of the dramatic context.

However, it is to be hoped that you will not be so unlucky as to have to contend with such outmoded views of theatre. You may rest assured that the majority of adults who make up your audience are there to be entertained willy-nilly, and can be guaranteed to enjoy your production regardless of all artistic criteria provided that it bears suitable evidence of their offspring's involvement. The parents in the audience are totally on the pupils' side, and can always be relied upon to respond enthusiastically whatever play you choose. (My own parents once travelled 400 miles to see me appearing as Oedipe in *La Machine Infernale*: and despite the fact that they speak little French, my presence in the cast was apparently enough to ensure their appreciation of a three-hour tragedy.)

To summarize:

You are looking for a play which has a theme which is accessible and relevant to your pupils; which has artistic integrity; which is immediate and vigorous with potential for plenty of movement; which will provide a good number of equally challenging roles for your best actors; which will provide opportunities for large numbers of children to participate to the level of their ability; which the children in the audience will find entertaining; and which will please the general public.

If you find a play that fully satisfies all these criteria simultaneously, please let me know. If you find a play that comes somewhere near to satisfying most of the criteria, you are as close as you are ever likely to get to finding the ideal School Play.

3 Choosing the play: different types of play

Having established the criteria upon which the choice of a play is to be based, your way is now clear to begin looking at actual plays. This chapter is intended to give a guide to the advantages and drawbacks of the various types of play that are available.

Shakespeare and the classics

I have already explained that to produce a Shakespeare play needs an exceptionally competent cast and an experienced director; and that I feel that it is not generally possible, in the average school, to do justice to the greatness of the plays. The same can be said of Shaw, of Ibsen and Tchekhov, of ancient Greek drama (with the exception of Aristophanes, the frankness and bawdiness of whose work may make him unsuitable for other reasons) and of most great drama which has a major verbal or literary content.

If, however, you feel that despite all the difficulties you have the confidence both in yourself and in your cast to go ahead with a 'classic' play, then I would recommend that you choose a play that deals mainly with the concerns of young people. This will lessen any trouble you may experience in convincing your pupil audience of the relevance of the play's theme to them; and it will make it easier for your cast to identify with the conflicts and situations of the play, thus allowing them to act with more inner conviction; and it will also lessen the chances of your stage being filled with adolescent boys with beards falling off their chins and clouds of talcum powder following them as they stagger and gibber in what they fondly believe to be the gait and speech of an old or middle-aged man.

To give but a few examples: it is far easier for young actors and actresses to identify with the young love of Romeo and Juliet than with the maturer passion of Antony and Cleopatra or the jealousy of Othello; and it is easier for them to understand and recreate the torments of Hamlet than those of Lear. The sentiments of most of

21

Shakespeare's comedies are probably more accessible: but here again young actors are more likely to be able to do justice to the feelings of the young lovers in *A Midsummer Night's Dream* than the middle-aged randiness of *The Merry Wives of Windsor*.

Figure 2

But please remember: it is better to be less ambitious and do it well, than to make mincemeat of a masterpiece. Or to put it another way, 'amateur drama is the art of the possible'.

Brecht and modern classics

The latter half of the twentieth century has produced a huge crop of fine plays and playwrights, many of whom bear witness to the towering influence of Bertolt Brecht. Among the works of Osborne, Pinter, Wesker, Shaffer, Stoppard – to name but a few out of the many excellent dramatists of their generation – can be found no shortage of plays which are already classics, and which combine literary and dramatic quality with a modern idiom and a modern approach to contemporary issues. In many cases a good play by an established living author will come closest to fitting the criteria listed at the end of the previous chapter.

Much modern drama has an immediacy and simplicity of style which appeals to young actors, and which can be traced directly to the influence of Brecht. The plays of Brecht himself, with their episodic structure, their clear-cut dramatic situations, their vivid everyday language, their opportunities for movement and crowd work, and their host of rewarding roles of all sizes, offer many excellent possibilities for a school play. In addition, the plays depend on a company approach, and Brecht's own theories of presentation mean that they can be produced on a low budget and with, if desired, a non-realistic design.

Plays written specially for children

You may decide – particularly if you are working with younger children – that any play written with adult performers and audience in mind is going to be too sophisticated. Many plays have been specifically written for children of different age groups, ranging from the simplest infants' nativity plays to the dramas written by Peter Terson for the National Youth Theatre. The Macmillan *Dramascript* series, which is expanding all the time, contains many excellent plays for children of secondary school age, including adaptations of many novels and short stories.

Beware of aiming too low. It seems to be a fact of child psychology that all children like to be thought of as more grown up than they really are. Young actors will generally be unhappy about playing roles of children younger than themselves, and will not hesitate to let you know indignantly if they find a play babyish. When asked to take a role in improvization most children will tend to choose to play a character a couple of years older than themselves: and in choosing a play written for children it may help to remember this preference.

The other danger of plays written for children or adolescents is that they often date very quickly, since playwrights frequently try to make their work appeal to young people by filling the dialogue with current slang. However, the problems of childhood and adolescence are universal, recurring in each generation; and provided it is not unduly dated, a good play on this theme may often be an ideal choice for a school play.

Historical plays

As well as plays about the problems of childhood, the gamut of plays written for children includes much material written with more conventionally educational aims, especially on historical themes.

We have already considered, when establishing our criteria, the relative importance of 'educational content' in the school play; and it is necessary to remember here that ultimately your production will be judged on its dramatic merits, and that the principal educational value of the play is as a complete project. However, if you can find an historical or otherwise didactic play with sufficient dramatic conflict and immediacy, and if you can satisfactorily solve the problems of period settings and costumes, you have the opportunity for a major undertaking in conjunction with the history department which will admirably fulfil many of our criteria.

The point about period settings and costumes must not be taken lightly: unless you have exhaustively researched the historical period in which your play is set you will let through niggling anachronisms upon which pedants will eagerly pounce; and if the historical content is integral to the theme of the play, then your usual excuses about dramatic reality and artistic licence will hold no water.

Modern experimental theatre

With the lifting of stage censorship, much modern 'fringe' theatre is probably too sexually explicit to be suitable for school plays. Not that your cast is likely to be offended or to raise any objections; but such subjects are generally too much for the delicate sensibilities of the average Head Teacher – or rather, the Head thinks, probably wrongly, that they are too much for the sensibilities of the average child and the average parent. In addition, to perform lines or actions of sexual explicitness requires a maturity of sexual experience which, according to traditional educational values, it is hoped your pupils do not possess.

However, it is a mistake to let the occasional four-letter word or sexual reference blind you to the dramatic merits – and in particular the dramatic inventiveness – of modern experimental theatre. Some experimental plays are pretentious and boring; others are unpleasant and shocking; but many are exciting and vivid, dealing with contemporary issues in a way that may be radical, but is not necessarily unsuitable for schools and schoolchildren. In particular, you may find that some modern plays offer exciting possibilities for dramatic use of large groups of performers, and for non-realistic styles of acting and presentation; and since, like you, most fringe theatre companies are working on an extremely low budget, you may gain many valuable ideas from seeing their work.

Musicals, operettas and rock musicals

If the involvement of vast numbers of performers is your top priority, then you may well be thinking of choosing a musical show. This will depend on your having already established a working partnership with a music teacher. (Although it would be just about possible for you to be both director and musical director, I cannot recommend this either for the artistic quality of the show or for your own health and sanity. Basically, it is very difficult for a musical director to get far enough away from a show to have the perspective necessary to be a satisfactory director.)

The first basic problem is the casting. Operettas and traditional musicals require real singers. In character roles you can generally get away with good actors who have mediocre voices; but every light opera or musical has a hero and a heroine – and probably numerous other characters as well – who have to sing well if the performance is not to fall flat. Moreover, it is unlikely that your best singers will also be your best actors: and this will inevitably lead to conflict between yourself and the musical director, and the eventual compromise of either the musical or the dramatic quality of the production. You may be lucky enough to have a number of pupils who can sing and act superbly; but find out before choosing a Gilbert-and-Sullivan or a romantic musical whether you have any tenors and basses with mature enough voices for solo roles.

Some schools solve this problem by giving all the principal roles to members of staff. This is generally fun for the staff, and conducive to a pleasant atmosphere in school since it allows pupils to see that the teachers are human. However, while this might be a good idea for a small-scale end-of-term romp, to produce a major show where the pupils merely take supporting roles and sing in the chorus while the staff act as stars is about as far as one could get from the spirit of the School Play as defined in Chapter One.

If you decide to produce a musical show, then it is far better to choose one which can be effectively sung by the sort of pupils you are likely to have in your cast. Most adolescents sound weak and uncomfortable in opera-style roles; but give them a microphone and a rock band to back them, and with a few simple lessons they can make an authentic and effective sound. Microphones are generally quite cheap to hire, and they can usefully get over the problem of the weakness of young voices; but they are only really visually acceptable in a rock-music setting. So it is worth considering the possibilities of making your show a rock musical.

The sound of rock music is one which will have instant appeal to a young audience; and with a rock opera you will have little difficulty in filling your auditorium with pupils at every performance. Moreover, if you are planning to use professional musicians to accompany your show you can get away with four or five players in a rock band; whereas most operettas and traditional musicals require a small orchestra, with consequent escalation of your budget. (If you prefer to use instrumentalists culled from the pupils and staff of your school, then still the chances are nowadays that you will find more competent players of guitars, drums and synthesizers than conventional orchestral instruments.)

The advantages of any musical show are that it offers scope for the involvement of huge battalions of pupils as dancers and/or vocal chorus (there is almost no limit: I once did a musical with a chorus of 150 singers and dancers); that the scripts of most musicals – especially rock musicals – involve considerable opportunity for exciting visual effects; and that most musicals – again especially those involving rock music – will be extremely popular, which will make cast recruitment and morale, as well as ticket sales, plain sailing. The disadvantages are the practical difficulties (which for the most part will be solved if you are working with a musical director, choreographer, and sound technician who know what they are doing); and the triviality of the plots of many musicals and rock operas; but you may well decide that these disadvantages are more than outweighed by the experience, for a very large number of pupils, of taking part in an ambitious, exciting, entertaining and successful show.

Variety and revue

If this is the first production you have attempted, you may feel that a revue of some sort is less ambitious than a play, and would therefore make a safer choice. It is certainly easier to organize rehearsals for a revue or a variety show, because you won't need the whole cast together so frequently. And if a member of the cast drops out, the whole show is not necessarily affected. Similarly, if some of the elements of your revue are badly performed, it doesn't ruin the entire evening. And finally, a variety show can contain dance, music, drama, poetry, comedy, acrobatics, judo, juggling, fire-eating – in fact anything at all at which a group of your pupils excel, and which you feel deserves an airing.

However, the other side of the coin is that a revue demands less from the performers than a play; and therefore it gives them less. Performing in a revue requires a style of acting more akin to showing off in front of an audience than involving oneself in a role, and may encourage the worst traits of self-indulgent actors. And because of the episodic nature of a revue, it does not generate the same spirit of group involvement as a play: each participant tends to think only of his part of the show.

A revue – if slickly linked and crisply performed – can be highly entertaining for cast and audience alike. Such an event might make a useful introduction in a school that has never put on a production before; but it is no real substitute for The School Play. And there can be few theatrical experiences more depressing than a bad revue – slow moving, full of weak and predictable jokes, and with lengthy pauses between acts. If you decide on a revue, it must be fast and funny, it must surprise the audience at every turn, and it must leave them wanting more.

If you have just read the whole of this chapter, you are probably feeling slightly more confused than you were ten minutes ago. However, I hope you will have narrowed the choice of play down to one category. If you are feeling energetic, you will now proceed to the Drama section of your local library and read dozens of plays until you find the right one; if you are feeling lazy you will turn to Appendix IV and make a choice out of the list of suitable plays which I have seen, read or directed; or perhaps, if you are still feeling at a loss, you will postpone your decision until you have read Chapter Four.

4 Alternatives to the written play

So far it has been assumed that you are looking for an existing scripted play. Before making your final choice, it may be worth considering a few alternatives to the whole idea. It would be possible to write a whole book on this subject but here there is just room to make a couple of brief suggestions.

Write your own play

If you are hoping to find a play with 29 speaking female roles and a part for a talented mimic with a stutter, then no amount of research in libraries is likely to help you. By writing your own play, you can solve this sort of problem by tailoring the material to suit your cast and resources: not only can you write with particular pupils in mind, but you can even build your ideas round the particular facilities of your hall staging arrangements.

If you have not written for the stage before, then the main point to remember is that theatre is primarily an audio-visual, not a literary medium. The simpler the words, the more effective your play is likely to be; and the most memorable theatrical moments are generally visual rather than verbal.

There are plenty of potential themes. You might take as your starting point a novel or a short story, or a historical event or period; if you want a musical show, then you could create a ballad-opera using traditional folk songs or any other type of music you are familiar with (I recommend, for example, the various folk-song collections of Roy Palmer as a basis for a musical-dramatic reconstruction of a historical period). Alternatively, you may decide upon a more contemporary theme, such as pollution and conservation, or an issue of particular local importance. Or else something from local history or folklore; or even a topic based upon some aspect of the curriculum – a scientific principle, the life of a poet or composer, or some aspect of moral education.

One of the most challenging possibilities is to choose a theme more directed towards your cast, such as the problems of the adolescent in society. Such a topic needs careful handling; but provided that you are in tune with the ideas of the children involved (a few discussion sessions might be useful before you put pen to paper) the potential is enormous. And should you wish to involve music or dance in your show, you will find that contemporary rock music offers no shortage of material on this theme, ranging from the Beatles' classic 'She's Leaving Home' to Pink Floyd's radical 'Brick in the Wall' which is number one in the charts at the time of writing.

An Improvised Play

The next logical step is to let your pupils create their own play through improvisation. This can be an intensely rewarding experience for all concerned; but I do not recommend that you attempt it unless you have some experience of working with children on improvisation.

There are several potential approaches, giving your pupils more or less freedom. A sort of half-way house is to present your cast with a list of scenes (any of the themes considered above would do), explain to them what happens in each scene, and let them fill in the dialogue by improvising. But far more satisfying is to let the whole idea come from the cast.

You will need to begin by getting your cast to select a theme. A certain amount of tactful guidance on your part will probably be necessary at this stage, or you will find yourself working on a production based on last week's episode of 'Kojak' or 'Star Trek'. Your cast may need to be reminded that live theatre is a very different medium from television, and it is neither practicable nor desirable for theatre to try to imitate television. If you jot down all the ideas suggested, and then chat about the potential for live theatre offered by each theme before any choice is made, your cast will probably choose the best one anyway.

Once a topic has been agreed upon, you will need to fill in some details. Of course, the choice of theme does not have to be final; and the cast must understand that the basis of improvisation is trust and experimentation, and the ideas they contribute are to be experimented on, tried out, and adopted, modified or rejected by the group as a whole. According to the type of theme, you may find it best to decide straight away upon a sequence of events and scenes, and then improvise to fill in the dialogue and action and test the dramatic potential of the ideas you have talked through. Or else you may decide to proceed by the method known as 'Instant Theatre' – a question-and-answer technique by which you ask questions, and the members of the cast raise a hand if they have an answer. In each case the answer supplied by the child you select is binding, and so elementary details can be filled in and the plot developed until you have enough material to proceed to improvisation.

But probably you will find it preferable to get the cast to improvise more freely upon aspects of the theme before any further group decisions are made. Any idea, however far-fetched, is worth exploring; and the eventual production will be the better if, for the first few sessions, no decisions are made other than the choice of basic theme, so that all avenues and possibilities can be freely explored, developed, and experimented with.

Gradually your show will take shape, with your cast fully involved with the production and direction of the show as well as the development of the drama. Specific workshop sessions on lighting, costumes and props will allow full collaboration on all the technical aspects of the play; and if it seems appropriate, sessions dealing with dance, music and masks can be added to give fresh ideas to the cast as they work on the production. Whether at any point you decide to write down the lines depends upon the type of situations that are developing: generally it will probably not be necessary.

To embark upon an improvised production is a brave step, requiring a great deal of confidence in yourself and in your cast. But if you can achieve the right creative relationship between yourself and the children involved, and you can come up with a play that works, the rewards for those concerned are higher than in any other type of School Play.

But enough of this theorizing. If you have read as far as this without having any idea as to what sort of play you wish to direct, then you had better return to Chapter One and start again. From now on I shall assume that your play is already chosen, and turn to the practical aspects of your role as its director.

5 Planning the production

Directing a play is a full-time job. You are trying to direct a play at the same time as teaching a full timetable. So before doing anything else you need to plan every aspect fully, so that you know what you are doing at every turn; and you need to secure promises of as much help as possible from your colleagues.

Involvement of other teachers

If this is your first production you won't yet know which of your colleagues you can rely upon; all you can do is try. If you can, find a named task for nearly every one of them: appoint a stage manager, a business manager, a publicity manager, a set designer with assistants, a lighting designer, a costume designer with assistants, a front-of-house manager, a production treasurer, a programme and ticket printing overseer, and any further officials you can think of. The chances are that you will still have to do most of the tasks yourself; but even if only two of the teachers you have cajoled end up doing the jobs they have volunteered for, it will have been worthwhile.

As soon as possible you will need a meeting of all the staff concerned with your production. At this you will need to outline the role to be played by each of your colleagues during the weeks leading up to the production, and to stress that in every aspect – even such unlikely elements as publicity and budgeting – pupil involvement should be as great as possible.

At this early stage you will also chat with all the heads of department whom you think you can interest in the idea of involving themes connected with the play in their syllabuses for the term. The English department may be able to study the text of the play or other works by the same or related authors. The history department may be able to study the period in which the play is set, or the history of theatre. If the action of the play takes place in a foreign country, the geography department may be able to study that country. The needlework, woodwork, metalwork, art and music departments may be able to base whole projects on the play. The maths and commerce departments may be able to involve the financial planning of the play in their work. The physics department may be able to study the electrical aspects of your lighting set-up. And all these departments of the school will be able to contribute to a display in the 'theatre foyer' (probably the classrooms adjoining the hall) on the nights of the performances, which will demonstrate the full involvement between the play and the school curriculum.

Knowledge of the text

Your own knowledge of the play must be extremely thorough. On first reading the script, try to be completely open-minded and unprejudiced, and to concentrate emotionally on the play, bringing to it sensations, pictures, memories, images, patterns and colours. On subsequent readings, consider the play in the light of the playwright's life and ideas – what impelled him to write it? And get a clear picture in your mind of the external facts of the skeleton of the play – the sequence of events seen from the point of view of each character. Then you will need to think about each of the characters in detail: his past and future, what makes him 'tick', and what are the motivations behind each of his actions in the play? Then you will need to study the style of the play – the use of language, imagery and symbolism, colour and rhythm; and the structure, harmony and pattern of the play's development.

Once you feel that you really know your play, and once your head is buzzing with images and ideas for your own production of it, you will need to discuss it in detail with those of your colleagues who are involved in the artistic side of the project – they will also need to have read the play and thought about it. In every case, the aim is to achieve the highest standard of work, consistent with involving the maximum number of pupils. Much of the potential value of the play is lost if the designing is all done by members of staff without the involvement of the children.

The acting space

Your first major planning consultation will be with the designer and the stage manager: and you will need to begin by deciding how best to use the resources of your school hall. Few schools possess a stage big enough to cope with a large-scale production; and even if your stage is huge, you need not feel obliged to use it. Placing young actors on a high proscenium stage removes the feeling of intimacy with the audience and introduces problems of projection. Moreover, it is a great help to pupils in your audience if you can transform the hall, so that the atmosphere is one of real theatre rather than of school assembly.

There are many ways in which you can utilize space for theatre: it is worth considering as many possibilities as you can before making up your mind. In particular, try to avoid placing chairs in straight rows, which generally results in the rear half of the audience being unable to see or hear, and those on the edges feeling left out of the ambience. And wherever possible try to make use of different levels – either by tiering up the seats, or by varying the level of the acting area, or both. The eventual format you choose needs to be practicable from the point of view of actors being seen and heard, of actors being able to enter and exit easily, of the audience being near fire exits and being comfortable, of any scene-shifting being simple, and of lighting being possible. Provided that all these criteria are satisfied, it is up to you and your designer to be as inventive as possible, and to devise a use of space that suits the mood of the play.

You might use three separate acting areas, with the audience in the middle, to make them feel caught up in the action. Or you might place the audience in a ring with the actors in the middle, so as to suggest that the actors are trapped, and to focus the audience's attention into one spot. Some plays need a feel of wide open space, others an atmosphere of claustrophobia. Sometimes you may wish to amaze an audience by placing an unexpected event behind them, or making a character enter from among them. The more inventive you can be in your use of space, the more help you are giving to the actors who will be using that space.

Set design

Your set can take the form of representational scenery; or something more abstract. In either case it is helpful to start with some idea of colour. Colours are highly emotive, and the predominant colour of your setting is going to make a major contribution to the atmosphere you create. Does the mood of your play as a whole demand gaudy fairground colours, or muted earthy shades, or sombre oppressive tones, or delicate pastel hues? And what colour changes between acts of your play will best serve to reflect the mood of each act and the relationships between the different sections of the play?

Some plays – especially most of those written between 1660 and 1914 – are most frequently performed using a naturalistic or representational set: indeed some writers, like Shaw, have sometimes written several pages at the beginning of each act describing every detail of the scenery visualized by the author. It must be remembered in such cases that the playwright obviously conceives his play as being performed according to the prevailing stage fashions of his time. Unless you are aiming for a production which sees the play purely as an historical statement – an attempt at a reproduction of the original production – you need not be afraid of considering modern and more experimental ideas for staging.

Figure 3 A two-dimensional football scene

A cut-out crowd, ball and grass tufts

You may in the end come back to representational scenery as being the best way of setting your play: but before making the decision, consider the possibilities of doing the play on a completely bare stage; of using mime, or two-dimensional cut-outs, (see Figure 3) instead of real furniture; of using abstract shapes and drapes and stark lighting to reflect the mood of the scene; of using a plain structure of scaffolding to represent different things in each scene (see Figure 4). Even if the text of your play demands windows, doors and fireplaces, there are other ways of creating these than purely representationally. A couple of rostrum blocks – or even a couple of chairs – can represent a window or fireplace in one scene, and then be transformed instantly into a tree or a wagon or a mountain for the next scene. An ornate fireplace or window-frame standing isolated on a bare stage can create the illusion of a whole room with solid walls, you can even use actors to represent scenery (see Figure 5) and

Figure 4
Use of scaffolding
In this scene the
Hunchback of Notre
Dame is pursued to
the bell tower.
Meanwhile Romeo
braves the balcony
whilst St Joan waits
in her cell below

furniture, so that two upright actors could be a door, and one crouched one a stool.

We tend to think of non-representational staging as a modern idea: and it is true that the influence of Brecht and his successors has made it an integral part of the theatrical style of the twentieth century. But it is worth remembering that Shakespeare had no elaborate scenery: for him a simple thrust stage with an inner curtained area and a small balcony could be turned instantly from

Figure 5
Actors as scenery
The human alphabet

the walls of Elsinore to Queen Gertrude's bedroom, and from a graveyard to a plain in Denmark, or anything else that the power of words and actions could suggest. To introduce complicated scene-changes into *Hamlet* would slow down the pace and rhythm of the play and clutter the action, by drawing attention away from the state of mind of the characters, which is where the drama is best focused, and towards the comparatively irrelevant physical situation. It is worth considering, even in a play that appears at first sight to demand a box set, the possibilities of speeding up the pace and focusing the audience's attention firmly onto the psychological drama by doing away with scenery altogether, or by reflecting the mood of the play in an abstract set design.

35

Costume and lighting

Once the setting of the play is planned, you will need to enter into similar consultations with the costume designer. The range of colours is equally important here. The costumes need to tone in effectively with the set, so that they also contribute to the mood of the set which you are striving to create; yet at the same time they must not blend in with the scenery, or the action will become difficult to watch. Relationships between characters can be suggested by colour: lovers should be in colours that complement each other, or else their embraces will be visually offensive; a character out of sympathy with the rest of the cast can be suggested by a costume the colour of which clashes with those of the other actors; the pomposity, simplicity, meretriciousness or carelessness of different characters can all be reflected in the style of their dress; and a character's change of mood can be reflected by a change of colour or of style in his costume.

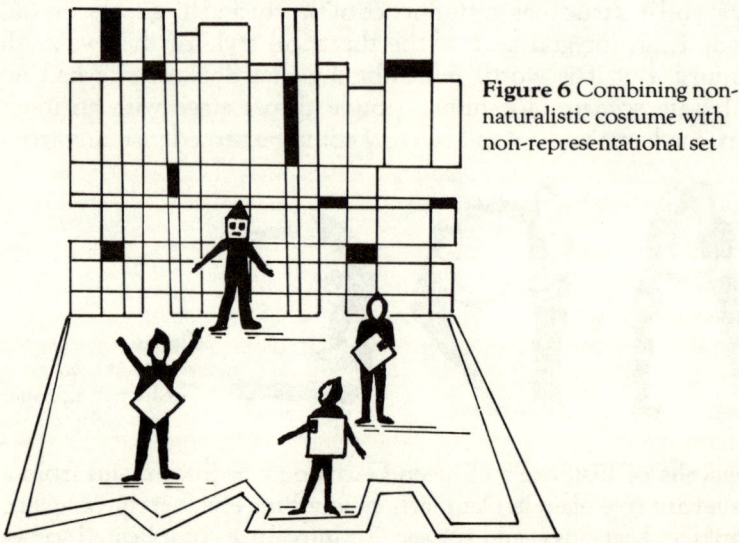

Figure 6 Combining non-naturalistic costume with non-representational set

As with scenery, it is worth considering the possibilities of non-naturalistic costuming (see Figure 6). If your setting is non-representational, you may be able to carry this style into the costumes – for example, all the cast could be dressed in black, as a sort of chorus, and each one could put on one additional garment, such as a hat, a coat, or a mask, whenever they assume a role. Or all the costumes could be grotesquely exaggerated so that the production takes on a surreal appearance; or a particular effect

36

could be gained by dressing all the characters as chess pieces, or clowns, or robots, or anything else that suits the style of the production; or their state of mind could be reflected in their style of dress, so that a self-righteous character wears a halo and wings, a fool wears a cap and bells, and an anxious and inhibited person appears tied up with string. As with the setting, the traditional naturalistic methods may well prove the best; but it is worth considering the possibilities of experimentation.

At about the same time in the production schedule you will need to talk to the lighting designer about what effects you would like. If you are hoping to include a disco-style scene, or a mime sequence with a strobe light to give a jerky 'silent movie' impression, or a realistic sunrise or fire or storm, then he will have to start experimenting straight away with what equipment the school possesses – and, if necessary, arranging to hire or borrow effects – wheels or special lanterns. Inventive use of lighting effects can transform a scene, so all possible ideas should be discussed, and their practicability assessed. What might be the effect of using low-level side-lighting for one scene, or doing another in silhouette against a purple cyclorama, or having different coloured gels in the lights to change the mood between scenes?

Crowd scenes

Even at this early stage you need to have thought hard about what each scene is going to look like – what colours are going to be involved, what sort of basic mood, and in particular what (if any) crowd or chorus scenes are you going to use. Crowds and choruses are an excellent way of involving large numbers of pupils to considerable dramatic effect; but they need to be very carefully planned, so that you know in advance how many performers you will need, what they will have to do, and how they will look. It is particularly disheartening for all concerned if large groups of children are called to lengthy rehearsals in order to practise standing motionless on stage while the principals deliver their lines; it is also particularly boring for an audience to have to watch such a crowd.

If you are going to place a crowd on stage, it must be doing something that contributes to the total dramatic effect: so you must plan from the start what sort of crowd they are to be. If you want a realistic 'straight' chorus – a crowd of bystanders – then every member of the group must have a character with his own actions and costume. The members of the crowd can generally find their characters through improvisation at an early rehearsal. Thus you can build up a naturalistic crowd that is interesting to look at because it is full of real people – fat mothers with disobedient children, vicars and gossips, vandals and hooligans, policemen and pickpockets, ice-cream salesmen and Salvation Army collectors, tight-trousered youths chatting up lipsticky girls. If your play demands a crowd – or even if it doesn't but you decide to insert one to provide comic relief from the main action or to cover a scene-change – then the crowd should be a major feature of the play, with interesting and realistic action from every member of it.

Figure 7 A choral group of indentical business men

Alternatively, you may decide on a non-realistic crowd: (see figure 7) a chorus of clowns or beggars to comment on a situation; a chorus of housewives or business-men, dressed identically, speaking chorally, and using an identical silly walk; a fire brigade forming a human fire engine, (see figure 8) or a chorus of soldiers

Figure 8 Human fire engine

entering as a human tank; a whole mime or dance sequence interpolated into a play so as to illuminate a dramatic situation, or act out the central character's dreams or nightmares.

Music

Any music you are planning to include needs to be thought of early as well. If your show is a musical, then you should be able to leave this to your musical director – provided that you are in basic agreement as to whether to employ professional musicians, or to use the talents of the school orchestra or any competent instrumentalists among your colleagues and pupils. If you do have a band of live musicians, it may be worth considering involving them in the action in some way, so that they represent a street band, a palm court orchestra, a glittery rock band or a heavenly chorus or whatever suits the play.

Even if your play is not a musical, a few live musicians can be a most dramatic addition – to create an atmosphere as the audience enters and during scene-changes; or to comment on the action throughout. (Anouilh uses this idea splendidly in *Le Bal des Voleurs*, where a solo clarinettist is on stage for much of the play, reacting to each character. There is no reason why this effect should not be borrowed for use in any other play.) A small percussion band can often be used to great effect, producing sound effects for battles or journeys, or providing rhythmic accompaniment to mime sequences or choral speaking.

Few adolescents are going to produce professional-standard acting (though with good training in a school where drama is an important part of the curriculum you hope they will come close to it); but there is no reason why your handling of stage space, scenery, lights, costumes, music and crowd scenes should be any less inventive than would be found in the National Theatre. All that is required is deep thought about the play, an inventive approach, and careful serious planning from the very beginning.

6 Casting

The first your pupils will know about the play is when they are invited to audition: so the way that you publicize the auditions is of great importance. A poster on the school notice board or a bill taped to the drama room window may attract those who are already keen, but will probably make little impact on the school as a whole. If possible, it is best to try to publicize the auditions personally, by addressing the whole school at Assembly, or better still by addressing smaller groups of children at house or year assemblies, where they will feel less bashful about asking questions.

The more lively you can make your address, the better. You should tell the children as much as possible about the play – the story, the background, the main characters, any appealing or lively production ideas you may have already devised, and all the different ways in which every pupil in the school can be involved. Right from the start, the pupils and the staff alike must receive the impression that the school play is not a highbrow diversion for a cultured elite, but a project involving every member of the school community. If the play is a musical, then try to play a few excerpts on record or tape – or better still, if you have the personal expertise, sing them yourself. Read sections from the play, so as to give the children the flavour of it. And try to tell them something of what is involved for the cast – the fun and enjoyment, but also the challenge and the personal commitment.

If you have done this job effectively, you may find that you have several hundred children wishing to be involved. This is a healthy and pleasing situation, but it makes your auditions even more of a nightmare than such events normally are. You want to choose the best performers for the main roles; but you do not wish to stunt the enthusiasm of all those who will not receive the main roles. If your play includes adequate opportunities for crowds and choruses, and you have carefully planned these elements of the production, you may be able to offer some sort of involvement to everyone;

otherwise you will have to be ruthless – perhaps cutting out all younger pupils who will have plenty more chances to take part in plays in the years to come.

If you are working in a single-sex school and you have chosen a mixed-cast play, then your best course is to try to team up with another school. The alternatives, with stages filled with actresses desperately trying to deepen their voices in counterfeit virility, or mincing half-broken-voiced actors tripping over sack-like skirts, bring with them too much embarrassment to bear contemplation. Adolescents are obsessively conscious of their developing sexuality, and to ask them to imitate the opposite sex in front of their friends is not only artistically unsatisfactory, but potentially socially excruciating for the children concerned. Whereas, for children reared in a single-sex establishment, the experience of collaborating with pupils from another school is likely to be both artistically and socially stimulating.

All actors dislike auditions: they are nerve-wracking for even the most experienced performer; and they involve a spirit of competition which is alien to real drama. But, unless you can think up a better method of selecting a cast, they are a necessity. To cast a play without auditions will bring justifiable suspicions of favouritism, and sour the atmosphere among your cast. (The only circumstances which might render formal auditions unnecessary are if your play derives from the activities of an existing drama club with whom you have been working for some time – so that you can make it clear that your casting decisions are based on what you already know of your pupils' abilities.)

You need to decide what qualities you are looking for in your cast, and devise audition exercises to try to find these qualities. I would suggest that your ideal school-play actor possesses eight specific qualities:

1 he shows sensitivity to others
2 he possesses the ability to project emotions
3 he is relaxed and uninhibited
4 he has a strong clear expressive voice
5 he moves well
6 he reads well
7 he is willing to be fully committed to the play
8 he will benefit from being in the play.

At some point before the final casting, all these eight qualities will need to be tested and compared. Which points you test in the preliminary auditions, and which ones you reserve for your final short-list audition, will depend partly upon the nature of the play (in a musical obviously the ability to sing and dance is of particular importance) and partly on how many children you are dealing with and how much time you have.

Your preliminary audition needs to contain a selection of different exercises. If you make the main activity reading from the play, then you will be selecting the best readers, who are not necessarily the most sensitive actors. A child with lots of personal talent – a fine voice, and the ability to move well – may not be a good choice if he is conceited, and lacks the ability to work well with others. A play's success depends upon the quality of the cast's co-operation more than on the individual talents of a few children. This is not to say that you are uninterested in talent or that you should never ask children to read; but the sort of audition one might use for adults, in whom the ability to read fluently is taken for granted, may not be appropriate for children.

If possible, do not have more than 20 children at an individual audition session, and take plenty of time over it, so that every child feels that he or she has been fairly considered. So if you have a hundred children wishing to take part, the preliminary auditions alone may need to be spread over a week – say an hour-long session after school each day. The following pattern is intended as an example of the sort of exercises you might devise, and *not* as a list of rules to be followed blindly through all auditions.

1 Give the children some warm-up exercises to get over the initial tension, and build up an atmosphere of group involvement. (See Chapter seven, section two, for some typical warm-up exercises).

2 Divide them into groups of four – preferably not with their own friends. (You will need to devise some simple system – eg giving each child a number – to select these groups; and you will need to be firm about it, as they will all complain bitterly when first separated from their friends. But working with friends is a less effective test of the child's sensitivity in acting, inhibits the development of a larger group identity, and usually produces a lower standard of acting because the children relate to each other as themselves rather than in role.)

3 Describe a situation (preferably one connected with the play) which the groups are to mime. If the children are unaccustomed to miming, demonstrate what is involved by showing them a piece of mime (not the same piece that they are

going to try, or they will all simply copy you). Give them two or three minutes to plan how they are going to tackle the subject, and then let each group in turn demonstrate the scene. The situation should be one that involves group concentration, co-operation, and physical exertion. The main aim of this exercise is to give the children something they can all do, and enjoy doing, which will give them some confidence. But during both the preparation time and the performance you will have the opportunity to note how each child reacts to the others, which children have the ability to move uninhibitedly, and which children are able to concentrate on a subject and 'believe' what they are doing.

4 Regroup the children – again insist that they follow your grouping rather than gravitating towards their friends – and then describe a situation (preferably from the play) which involves a selection of distinct and equally-weighted characters. The children are to improvise this situation using dialogue and movement. Three or four are the best numbers for a group: if you have the groups any larger the shyer participants are liable to get neglected. If the children are unaccustomed to improvisation, demonstrate (perhaps with another member of staff) what it entails; once more, do not demonstrate the 'set' scene, or all the children will try to copy you. Depending on the nature of the scene and the experience of the children a further warm-up, perhaps involving lights or music, might be useful to help build up the atmosphere. The groups will then be given five minutes or so to prepare the situation; and after this each group will show something of what they have prepared. During the preparation period (which may take considerably longer than five minutes) you will be trying to see how the children are reacting to each other – which ones are producing ideas, and which ones are blocking other people's ideas and trying to ensure that they emerge as 'stars'. If it goes well, this exercise as a whole should give you enough information as to the children's general ability to enable you to select your short-list. If you wish to test the children's reading ability as well at this stage, you may wish to add a reading exercise, as follows.

5 Regroup the children, and give each child a copy of the play, or some duplicated simplified excerpts. (You will have previously selected a scene involving three or four equally weighted characters.) You will need to give the children a little time to prepare the scene, so that those with reading problems

can work out their lines; then let each group in turn read out the scene.

You will have noticed that throughout this sample audition I have set group activities rather than individual audition pieces. I cannot sufficiently stress that you are looking for talented children who can co-operate sensitively, not budding 'stars'. Right from the start of the first audition, the children should be aware that a play is a group activity, not an opportunity for ego-exposure.

The preliminary auditions will no doubt already have given you a few ideas as to who might be suitable for particular roles. For the final audition you will require all the short-listed applicants together, so that you can try out different combinations until you find the best one. At the beginning of the final audition it is worth emphasizing the degree of commitment you will require from your cast. If any of the auditionees have other strong commitments (eg public examinations or sports) or are uncertain about whether they are really interested in the play, it is better to talk over their problems now rather than later.

Exactly what goes into the final audition depends completely upon the play. I would suggest that it involves both the improvisation and the reading of scenes and situations from the play, with everybody having the opportunity to try a wide selection of characters, until finally you are convinced that you have chosen the best possible cast.

The last of the eight qualities I have suggested that you are looking for in your actors is the one which most distinguishes your role as director of a school play from that of the director of a professional company: your ideal actor is the one who will most benefit from being in the play. The school play is an educational as well as an artistic venture, and in the last resort your casting must take into consideration not only the excellence of the performers you are choosing, but also the social and educational needs of each individual child.

In certain cases – I will give but a few examples – your casting decisions may become extremely complex. You may need to decide – probably in consultation with those teachers who know the child best – whether giving a major role to a particularly sensitive child will give that child the confidence to reveal and exploit his potential more fully in all aspects of his life; or whether it will provide a burden of worry over line-learning and rehearsal attendance that will hamper his development. You may have to decide whether to give a leading role to a child who has already proved himself in major roles in previous plays; or whether to choose a child who, though less talented, has shown particular devotion and enthusiasm which you would like to foster. You may need to decide whether a child from a comparatively deprived or uncultured background might derive more benefit from a major role than the child of highly educated parents for whom theatre and the arts are already an important part of life. And you may need to decide whether the role of a bullying loud-mouthed character is best given to a child who possesses these qualities in real life and might see in the role a glorification of his conduct; or to a quieter child who might not give such a convincing performance in the role, but who might gain confidence from attempting a role alien to his natural temperament.

This leads on to the whole question of the virtues of type-casting as opposed to casting against type, over which directors in all aspects of theatre will always continue to argue. In a school play, which is designed to be an educational experience for all concerned, and in which the social well-being of the cast as pupils is a part of your concern, the argument is particularly important. My own reaction has generally been to cast against type wherever possible. Children are naturally self-conscious, and harm can sometimes be done by asking them to face up to and expose the qualities of their own personalities and appearances.

To give one obvious example, if a character is supposed to be ugly, it would generally be insensitive in the context of a school play to give that role to a girl who is lacking in confidence about her appearance, and whose self-confidence might be increased by the reactions of her friends seeing her in that role. If, however, the part of the ugly character is given to an attractive and confident girl, she is likely to give a better performance because whe will be more prepared to behave as if she is ugly, being uninhibited by the fear that the audience are seeing herself, and not the character she is playing, as being ugly. In addition, her exploration of the character of someone who is physically ugly may help an attractive child to avoid the conceitedness that so often afflicts people who are told too often that they are beautiful.

The same argument applies to most character traits. Paradoxically, it is often easier for a young actor to portray a character markedly different from himself than to play a character similar to himself, since the latter involves a degree of self-knowledge that few adolescents possess, and a degree of self-exposure that most adolescents would be embarrassed by.

These points are all somewhat delicate, since obviously they cannot be discussed with the children involved. As far as the children are concerned, the auditions must be seen to be scrupulously fair, and your decisions must be understood to be based purely on the artistic considerations of the best combination of actors. But with a school play, there is always a social, non-artistic aspect of your role as director. Once the rehearsals are under way, you will be working in close contact with a group of enthusiastic children, and you will inevitably find that, as they stretch and explore their personalities through their roles under your guidance, you are getting to know them far better than you normally have the opportunity to know children you teach. You are getting to know them informally, outside the necessary discipline of the classroom; and thus you are in a position to understand and assist in their social development in a way which few schoolteachers are able to attain.

This can be one of the most rewarding aspects of teaching, when the conventional roles of teacher and pupils are relaxed in a spirit of group involvement, so that they see you and you see them as complete human beings, aside from the poses into which the educational system as a whole tends to force both teachers and pupils. It is a privilege and a responsibility which should not be taken lightly.

7 Rehearsals: the preparation

If this is the first school play you have produced, you may naively suppose that organizing the early rehearsals is simply a question of listing the characters in each scene, then calling rehearsals for a scene at a time in dinner-hours and after school at your own convenience. Unfortunately such an ideal scheme is only practicable if as well as being the producer of the play you are also the Headmaster or at least a deputy head. For any lesser member of staff, organizing rehearsals is an exasperating exercise in juggling between all the conflicting activities and priorities that fill up children's lives.

Preliminary frustrations

Inevitably the child playing Macbeth is required after school every Monday and Wednesday for football practice; Lady Macbeth has ballet lessons every Tuesday and extra French every Thursday; and the Headmaster has put Banquo in detention every Friday for smoking in the toilets. So you have to begin carefully explaining to your cast that being in a play is a major commitment for each of them, involving responsibilities to the school as a whole and the rest of the cast in particular. It will also be necessary to explain – for the benefit of lazy optimists – that being in the play will not be considered an acceptable excuse for failure to do maths homework.

Assuming all your cast are prepared to make this commitment of their time, you then have to placate – or negotiate a compromise with – all the teachers of after-school activities whose sessions are going to be depleted by the absense of your cast during rehearsals. This usually results in some complex system by which you are to have Hamlet every second Wednesday provided that you allow him home early on evenings before away matches and provided that he behaves himself in chemistry for the rest of term.

Having sorted all this out, you will then discover that Ophelia lives ten miles away and can only get home by the school bus which leaves immediately after school, while Gertrude cannot rehearse during dinner hours because she has to go home and collect her baby brother from play school. Ophelia's problem can usually be solved by finding someone – probably a member of staff – in fact probably you – who can drive her home after the rehearsal. Gertrude's problem may well be insuperable: but it's worth trying to get her to get one of her friends to look after baby brother for the more vital dinner-time rehearsals. Incidentally, it is probably worth sending a note to the parents of your cast at about this time, to ensure that they are aware of when the performances are to take place, and roughly when the regular rehearsals will be. You cannot rely on the children to know when they are going to be on holiday or moving to another school. In one of my productions, a girl in a fairly major part failed to appear for the first performance: it turned out that her parents were completely unaware that their daughter was involved in a play, and had decided to keep her at home that night for some minor domestic transgression.

Now that you have – with luck – secured the availability of at least some of your cast for at least some of your rehearsals, your next task is to work on securing the availability of the rehearsal space. Early rehearsals can possibly be taken in your own classroom (or – if you are really lucky – drama studio). But once you are dealing with the chorus, or you are rehearsing anything involving stage movements, you probably need to be in the hall. And at this point you find out that the girls' PE department wants the hall whenever it rains, the Deputy Head is filling it with desks for a fortnight of mock exams, and the Headmaster needs it for a Governors' Meeting and a parents' reports evening in the week of the dress rehearsal. How you solve these difficulties depends on your status in the staff. If you are the Deputy Head, then you simply publish a list of your rehearsal times on the staff-room notice board and close your office door behind you. Otherwise, your best bet is to try to avoid clashes as tactfully as possible and as early as possible by friendly chats with the Head of PE, the conductor of the school orchestra, and any other regular users of the hall. But at the same time make sure that if clashes do occur, you win them: be firm in your insistence that the school play is important, that you must have the space to rehearse, and that – your strongest card – it is only for a few weeks and then the play will be over. If the Head of PE still proves recalcitrant, then wait till the school football team wins a game, buy him a drink, and ask him again.

Having squared your staff colleagues by fair means or foul, your hardest – and in many ways most important – task still remains. Rehearsals after school, lights on the lighting bars, scenery on the stage: all these involve a break in routine. And the minutest divergence from the normal school routine is anathema to the school caretaker. Immense care and tact is required in this most delicate and vital area: indeed, how he handles the caretakers is what most distinguishes the seasoned producer of the school plays from the raw novice. You have only got to get on the wrong side of one caretaker, and your rehearsals are doomed from the start. You and your cast will be kept waiting 20 minutes while the floor dries before you are allowed into the hall. You will find yourself banished from the hall altogether because the chairs are already set out for tomorrow's assembly. You will not be allowed to open the door to the stage wings because, in the words of one caretaker, 'unlocking doors spoils the school's security'; and on the dot of 4.55 pm your rehearsal will come to an abrupt end as the lights flash on and off – and any word of protest will draw forth a complete inventory of everything the zealous caretaker has had to do since he arrived to stoke the boilers at six that morning.

But with the aid of a few cans of lager (or in really stubborn cases a small bottle of Scotch), and your tacit agreement that the caretakers are the most sensible and important members of the school community, none of this need happen, and your rehearsals can run like clockwork. The drink may cost you a couple of pounds, and your acquiescence in their view of their status may cost you a few ounces of pride; but if the school caretakers are on your side, then a huge weight is off your mind, you can be sure that the hall will be available whenever you want it, and you may confidently proceed to your first rehearsal.

The warm-up

Half the cast are sitting huddled in their coats looking exhausted after the school day. The other half are chasing each other up and down the hall and fighting. Your first task is to turn the atmosphere into one of alertness and concentration. Start by making sure that the friends of the actors aren't jeering at them through the windows – or, worse still, have come to watch the rehearsal. Then you need to lead a sequence of activities involving everyone present – including stage hands, prompters, etc – designed to focus the attention of your company, alert their minds and bodies, and relax them ready for acting. (It is important that you do not allow anyone to watch the warm-up without participating: otherwise its effect may well be to generate more selfconsciousness than it dispels.) Depending on the children, and your relationship with them, the aims of the warm-up can be achieved by using games, or exercises, or both. There are many drama games to choose from, and each one has a specific purpose – to exercise the body, to focus group attention, to break down inhibitions, to build up trust between the participants, to accustom children to role-playing, etc. You will be able to devise specific games designed to prepare children for coping with particular problems that arise in the play you are dealing with. What games you use will depend on your own judgement of the needs of the cast – whether they need waking up, calming down, or what. Generally I have found that games go better – increasingly so as children get older – if you explain the serious purpose behind each game, so that they are not seen as a giggle or a waste of time.

Within the confines of this book it is not possible to describe in detail the dozens of games of different types that are effective for drama. If you are stuck, a look through a selection of the books listed in Appendix III should give you some ideas. As an alternative to – or in addition to – a selection of drama games, the warm-up can be done through a sequence of simple physical exercises. The sort of exercise sequence I generally take a cast through is the same type of sequence that I use myself, as an actor, before going on stage. Again, I find that it works better if I explain to the cast why we are doing it, and what is the specific purpose of each exercise.

I divide my exercises into two categories: those designed to wake the body up, and those designed to relax it. As actors we are trying to convey character and emotion to an audience by means of our bodies: and so we need to have complete awareness and control of all the parts of our bodies, and we need to be relaxed so as to get away from all the mental and physical tensions that come from self-consciousness, and the personal mannerisms (shuffling from foot to foot, brushing hair off the forehead, etc) to which we all unconsciously resort.

I usually begin my waking-up (or 'awareness') exercises with the hands and feet, and then work through all the parts of body, bringing to life and loosening up each area in turn until the whole body is alert. Begin by waggling the fingers or trying to shake them off the hand; then try to shake the hand off the wrist, and the arm off the shoulder. The same can be done with toes, ankles, knees and hips; and finally all four limbs can be shaken vigourously like a string puppet controlled by a demented puppeteer. If this is done effectively the tingling of the blood in the fingers and toes can be distinctly felt. Gentler alternatives to the energetic shaking movements are a more controlled circling of fingers, hands, lower arms, and complete arms, followed by toes, feet, calves and complete legs; or else a curling and stretching sequence with the whole body. moving from a central curled position to extend the body upwards, forwards, backwards, left and right.

After the limbs are exercised, the central parts of the body need to be similarly awakened. The stomach muscles can be toned up by touching toes then standing up straight, or by trunk curls (the same exercise done lying down); and the sides can be stretched by reaching the right hand down the right leg and likewise with the left side. Circling or shaking of the pelvis is a good exercise, but will produce giggles and embarrassment if your cast don't yet know each other well, and so is best left out of the early rehearsals. The shoulders – generally the stiffest part of any self-conscious child – can be raised and lowered and circled one at a time then both together ('the Edward Heath exercise' – interestingly, few children are now aware that Mr Heath was once Prime Minister, but every child knows that he is supposed to waggle his shoulders.) Finally, the neck needs to be loosened by rolling the head round in both directions, and the features of the face to be awakened by wiggling in turn everything that wiggles – nose, cheeks, jawbones, eyes, eyebrows, lips. After all these exercises, a general loose jog or shake completes the awareness of the whole body.

I generally follow these 'waking-up' exercises with two basic relaxation exercises. For the first, the feet are placed slightly apart, and then the children imagine that from the waist down they are made of concrete, while from the waist up they are a rag doll or puppet made of some floppy material, and attached to the roof by a string from the back of the neck. On a given signal the string is released so that the top half of the body flops to the floor and the head and arms dangle lifelessly. Then the string is very gradually drawn back up, so that the body is pulled upright with the arms and head still hanging floppily. As the body comes upright the head rolls into place on top of the spine and the shoulders 'click' back into place – thus producing a relaxed comfortable stance that it is impossible to achieve by telling a child 'just stand normally'.

For the second relaxation exercise, the cast lie on their backs on the floor with their hands by their sides. Then they go through each part of the body in turn, first clenching it tightly, then relaxing it as much as possible: toes, feet, calves, thighs, buttocks, stomach, fingers, hands, arms, shoulderblades, neck and face. At the end of this the whole body should be completely relaxed; and the warm-up session can conclude with a minute or so of silence, lying relaxed, concentrating on the points where the body is touching the floor, or on the slow steady rise and fall of the breathing.

This last exercise is as much concerned with mental as with physical relaxation (although the children, especially if young, do not necessarily need to be told this). Consequently, it is worth taking a little trouble to create the right atmosphere, so as to try to avoid distractions and giggles. I have known children feel embarrassed by the vulnerability of their position in the last exercise (on their backs with eyes closed) especially when the exercise is led by a teacher of the opposite sex. It is to be hoped that after the first couple of rehearsals such tensions will have dissolved in a general spirit of communal trust; but, especially with adolescents, this sort of problem needs to be taken into account. The calmness and confidence in your voice as you take the exercise will help; an intelligent explanation of the purposes behind the exercises will also help; and, if possible, I think it is a good idea if you yourself do whatever you ask the children to do. If they can see you doing the exercises then they have a strong lead – and the question of you making them look foolish will not arise.

It must be stressed that the exercises I have described are intended as examples of a suitable warm-up sequence, rather than a definitve list every director must follow before every rehearsal. What is important is that at the end of the warm-up you have a united, alert, relaxed cast: how this is to be achieved will differ greatly from school to school and from rehearsal to rehearsal. The exercises do not need to be at all strenuous – they can be quite gentle if you like: or else more energetic if the cast seems particularly lethargic one day, or you need to have them fit for some lively dance or fight sequence. The way that you present the exercises can vary too: sometimes musical accompaniment can help to establish rhythm or atmosphere; sometimes they can be done in complete silence as a follow-my-leader routine, with the cast imitating all of your actions. Once the cast understand the reasons for the exercises, and have come to appreciate their efficacy, then members of the cast can take over from you to lead the exercises.

Some rehearsals are snatched during odd half-hours at dinner-time, and it may not be practical to spend 20 minutes – or, indeed, any time at all – warming up. But for all major rehearsals, a warm-up session of games or exercises is very useful, and there is no other way of getting your cast as a whole into the right frame of mind for good acting.

The warm-up can be quite long for the first few rehearsals, until a group identity and trust is built up. Then perhaps five or ten minutes will be enough to achieve the necessary concentration, alertness and relaxation. But it is well worth while continuing right through your rehearsal schedule to start every main rehearsal with some sort of group exercise, so that when it comes to the first night you have a ready and familiar method of calming stage nerves and preparing the cast – both mentally and physically – for the rigours of the actual performance.

Learning lines

It will help a lot if your cast know well in advance which rehearsals they will be needed for. So quite early on – having checked with the cast for occasions when they know they are going to be unable to attend because of outings, exams, etc – it is a good idea to issue a duplicated rehearsal schedule, showing which scenes you plan to rehearse on which days. Also on this schedule you will include deadlines for the use of props, costumes and lights, and the learning of lines for each scene.

Line-learning is a major worry for children. As a professional actor visiting many schools, I find that one of the most frequent questions children ask me is 'How did you manage to learn the lines?' If you have adequate rehearsals, learning of lines should not be a problem. By the time of the deadline, your cast should have been through every scene so many times that they more or less know the lines anyway, and it will require little effort to fix the words firmly in their minds. If any of your cast still have trouble remembering what they have to say, the best way to learn lines is with a cassette tape recorder: first the actor should make a recording of the complete scene and listen through it until he thinks he knows it; then he should make a recording of the scene leaving pauses in place of his own lines, so that he can play it through and practise saying his own lines in the right places.

But it is better, if possible, to allow the lines to be learnt gradually in the course of rehearsal. If you make your cast 'cram' their lines too quickly, then they will tend to think of them purely as lines, and will find it far more difficult to make their characters believable, to 'feel' the reasons and emotions behind the lines, and to speak the lines as if they are the result of those emotions rather than vice versa. Plenty of rehearsal will mean that the lines gradually become familiar as part of the scene and of the character, and they will not be easily forgotten; whereas if they have been learnt 'cold', out of the context of the rehearsals, the young actor is far more likely to forget them when he has to contend with stage nerves at the first performance.

8 Rehearsals: directing the play

As the play's director, you have four main tasks to accomplish during the course of the rehearsals: to establish the emotional and dramatic centre of each scene; to arrange the timing, balance, pacing and climaxes so that the dramatic effect is at its maximum; to organize the grouping and movements of your cast so that the action is clear and dramatic and never awkward; and to teach your pupils how to act, and coach them in their individual roles.

Simultaneously with all this, you have to maintain the cast's morale, look to the problems of individual children who get 'bogged down' by difficulties in learning lines or attending rehearsals, and continue to supervise all the backstage activities – preparation of scenery, costumes, props, lights and make-up – and the offstage activities – advertising, ticket sales, finance, and public relations within the school and within the staff-room. The whole operation, when carried on at the same time as teaching a full time-table, is rather like juggling with about eight medicine-balls.

Analysis of scenes

Your first couple of rehearsals, following the warm-ups and introductory exercises, will probably take the form of read-throughs, so that your cast can get used to the structure of the play as a whole, and the roles that they are to play.

You will find that most children begin with an undue reverence for the written text, and a complete disregard for the dramatic meaning of the lines. The notions of irony and subtext – which are crucial to the interpretation of most plays – will probably not occur to them unaided. And so, right from the early read-throughs, and as a continuing process throughout the rehearsals, you must lead discussions involving the active and constructive analysis of each scene, so that the cast learn to think about the emotions and reasons behind each line they have to say. Does the character really mean what he says? Or is he being sarcastic or ironic? Or is he trying to deceive the other characters? Or is he deceiving himself? Or is he speaking under duress caused by his anger or fear or grief or love or jealousy? Each line needs to be analyzed in this way at some point in the rehearsals. Then the part played by each character needs to be analyzed over the course of the whole scene. How does the character feel at the start? How does he react to each of the events of the scene? How do his emotions change and develop during the scene? At what precise points do his feelings start to alter? How does he feel by the end of the scene?

Sensible discussion of each of these topics should lead each pupil to understand what his character is doing in each scene, and therefore to 'live' through the scene, reacting believably to each event, rather than standing dumbly through other people's speeches and only switching himself on for his own lines. Thus the lines will eventually be spoken as a result of the emotions felt by the characters, rather than the emotions being tacked on to the lines as a sort of afterthought.

As the director, your own deep analysis of the play as a whole will lead to your final decisions as to how each scene can be played. According to how you direct the scene, and how you see the scene as fitting into the structure of the play as a whole, the events can be seen from the point of view of one character or another, and the sympathy and attention of the audience can be wherever you choose to focus it. From the basis of the artistic view of the play as a whole which you have acquired, you will need to explain to your cast what you see as the fundamental dramatic reason behind each scene. Why did the dramatist write this scene? Why did he place it in this particular position in the play? What do we wish the scene to show? Are there themes, images, or ideas buried in this scene that connect it to other scenes, or that we particularly want to bring out as part of our general interpretation of the play? Once the cast have all read and thought about the play, they should feel confident to put forward their own ideas as to artistic harmony and subtext, and your rehearsals will include some lively and intelligent discussion, to the enrichment of the whole cast's understanding of the play.

As well as discussion, you may find it extremely helpful to use improvisation to develop your cast's understanding of the characters they are playing and the scenes they are enacting. What was the central character like as a child? What will he be like in old age? How might any of the characters have developed the personalities which they have acquired by the time of the action of

56

the play? How would some of the characters react to situations other than those they encounter in the course of the play? What might happen if a scene turned out differently: if a character refused to yield to persuasion, or yielded more easily? Or if a character were to react more or less sympathetically than the way he reacts in the text? With the use of improvisation topics like these, your cast will with luck come to believe in the characters as real people, and will learn to perform each scene as if it is really happening, rather than as a predestined sequence of events.

Timing, balance, pacing and climax

A play is an audio-visual, not a literary, event. And so your handling of the rhythms and climaxes of every scene is of vital importance. It is for this that a director is most necessary: just as the musicians in an orchestra need a conductor to unify the ensemble, establish the speeds, coordinate the interpretation of the score, and organize the balance so that every note is heard; so the actors in a play need a director to make the decisions that will unify and balance the performance and coordinate the group interpretation of the text. It is not possible for the members of the cast to do this, because only the director can see the play as a whole.

From your analysis of each scene you will have decided what you see as its climax. Often the climax of a scene will not be a verbal one – it might be a look, a laugh, a shriek, an embrace, a slap or a stamp. Once you have decided on your climax, the whole scene needs to be orchestrated so as to build up to that moment. The movements and groupings of the characters, the handling of lights and sound, and the pace and pitch of the lines must all lead towards your climax, so that the scene as a whole has a balance, a shape, and a purpose.

The timing of individual lines is something that may come naturally to some children. It is your task to build up a rapport among your entire cast so that the sense of timing becomes a group feeling. In comedy timing is very important, and its effect is obvious: a line will fall flat if wrongly timed, and will be funny if correctly timed – sometimes yielding two or three laughs from the perfect positioning of looks associated with it. In more serious scenes the timing is no less important, but its effect is more subtle. Frequently looks, pauses, and moments of stillness will be the most effective moments in a scene: it is your responsibility to arrange these so that the dramatic effectiveness of the scene is at its maximum.

At the same time, you must keep a control over all the

performers, so that none are over-acting or overdoing the pauses to the detriment of the scene as a whole. Just as the second-trombone-player would have difficulty in judging his volume unaided, so each actor needs to be told where to underplay, where to overplay, and where to hold back so that another character can become dominant. With a bit of luck you will succeed in fostering a group sensitivity among your cast, so that none will be tempted to over-act, because all are aware of the dramatic purpose of the scene.

The pacing of the scene is not quite the same as the timing: the timing is concerned with individual moments and lines, while pacing deals with the rhythm of the scene as a whole. Which sections of the scene should be slowed down so as to build up tension and suspense, or because they contain essential information that the audience might otherwise miss? Which sections need to be speeded up so that the scene will not drag, or so as to create an atmosphere of urgency? Will your climax be emphasized by a speeding up or a slowing down? Where will the dramatic quality of the scene be enhanced by an atmosphere of calm, of frenzy, or of grandeur? What minor climaxes will you introduce to lead up to the main climax and bring out the important themes of the scene? Like the punctuation in a paragraph, the pacing of the scene must at all times make the meaning clear, and introduce enough variation to hold the audience's attention.

The pitch and volume of the scene are also under your control. Which sections of the scene would be more effective if shouted – or whispered? Which sections need strong movements, and which would benefit from stasis? Which moments need to be emphasized by loud voices charged with emotion, and which by quiet intensity or introspective soliloquy? Which lines should be spoken aside, or treated lightly as 'throw-aways'?

Most children will begin by assuming that there is only one correct way to say the lines, and only one correct way to move. All the final decisions as to climaxes, timing, balance, pacing and volume must be yours: but the play will be more effective both artistically and educationally if the cast have participated in the making of your directorial decisions, and understood the reasons for each decision. Preliminary exercises, such as taking a line or group of lines and getting each member of the cast to say them in a different way, will help to show your cast how varied are the possible interpretations of each line. And it may be useful to rehearse whole scenes in completely different ways – with a different character dominant each time, or different sections loud or soft, fast or slow, or acting the scene in the style of melodrama or vaudeville or any other particular style – so that your pupils are aware of the hundreds of possibilities, and feel that they are participating in the group interpretation of the script, and not merely doing blindly what the director tells them.

Grouping and movement

Some plays are published with comprehensive stage directions printed in the text. It is your own decision whether you follow these or not. In a Beckett play, for instance, to omit a pause or change a move might affect a whole scene; but in many plays, to ask an actor to recite a speech while slavishly following a printed stage direction like 'He crosses DR, picks up book, returns UC, sits opens book, and looks up' will destroy any of the integrity of character and action that you and the actor have been striving to build up.

If a character is going to make a move, it must be because that character instinctively makes the move; not because the director or the printed text has told the actor that the character should move. As director you will suggest moves to your actors, so as to maintain a pleasing and effective grouping, to eliminate any awkwardness in necessary stage business, to avoid characters masking or upstaging each other, and to present a varied and harmonious spectacle to your audience. But although you as the director will suggest the moves, it must be the characters – not the actors – who make them. Every movement must have a reason, and it must be made in character: it is always painfully obvious if an actor is moving as an actor, rather than in role.

In every scene, the movements must contribute to the total dramatic effect, so that the focus of the audience's attention is where you wish it to be, and movements do not distract from the scene's tension or climax. To make every move work dramatically and at the same time keep every movement in character takes a certain amount of skill and practice in the director; but the early rehearsals are for experimentation. So try rehearsing some scenes with different amounts or types of movement, so that your cast can see all the various possibilities, and can see how you come to the final decisions as to who moves where and how.

All of us have our own nervous mannerisms, which tend to become particularly prominent when we know we are being watched. Your actors – especially the less experienced ones – will unconsciously shuffle from foot to foot, straighten their jumpers, brush their hair out of their eyes, twist their hands together, and indulge in a whole gamut of nervous fidgets of which they are probably quite unaware. Your opening warm-up exercises should remove much of the physical tension and nervousness; but you will find that your cast needs practice even in something as simple as standing still on stage. They will only be able to move in character if they have successfully abandoned their own personal mannerisms: so you may find it helpful to get them to improvize – or rehearse scenes from the play – in complete stillness, and then to practise walking, sitting and moving as their character, before attempting to fix the moves which they will eventually make on stage.

With chorus or crowd scenes, movements must be a little more prepared and pre-organized, so that the children know what they are to do, and the rehearsal is not too messy. To create the effect of a naturalistic crowd, improvisation is essential: each group within the crowd works out its own business, and then you position the groups so as to produce a harmonious effect. With non-naturalistic chorus movement, once again it is preferable to let the members of the chorus participate in the experimentation, so that they understand what is their dramatic function, and why they are being asked to move in a stylized way.

Some stage movements will need specific separate rehearsal – notably any stage fights. Children love stage fights, and you will probably find that they produce many inventive ideas of their own. It is important to distinguish between a real fight – which is generally messy, boring and unpredictable – and a stage fight, which must be fast-moving and uncluttered but which can be extremely spectacular. Many of the combat sports – boxing, wrestling, and especially judo and karate – are extremely dramatic in themselves. You may well find that some of your pupils have some knowledge of these; and for a major stage fight it may be worth calling in an expert on judo, karate or fencing. You will find children remarkably athletic and resilient, and with a bit of care you will be able to create a fight involving magnificent throws and falls. If your acting area has different levels, fighters can leap on each other from above or fling each other down. Children will delight in simulating real injury by kicking the floor beside a body or whacking the floor with a stick: both techniques can look horrifyingly realistic if accompanied by the shrieks, groans and writhings of the 'victim' and done at high speed. Stage blood – taped to the body in a polythene sachet which is pierced by a pinpoint on a ring – can add gruesome realism if such is the style of your production.

In fights, as in all stage movements, I have always found it preferable to approach a rehearsal with plenty of ideas, but to involve the cast themselves in the experimentation and in the actual choice of the sequence of moves and events. This makes the preparation of the play far more of a creative experience for your pupils than if they merely have to obey unquestioningly the instructions given by yourself or by the book.

Acting technique

For children who have little experience of acting, there is a bewildering amount to be learnt. You will probably find that some, if not all, of your cast require individual or small-group coaching in acting technique.

Some children will be particularly awkward and uncoordinated in their movements: and to draw attention to this in a full rehearsal might increase those children's self-consciousness and make the problem worse, as well as wasting the time of the rest of the cast. You will probably find it helpful to arrange a separate time to take a small group of these children through extra exercises – warm-up and breathing exercises to try to reduce tension, and then exercises to develop physical balance and control, and to practise walking, sitting and standing without awkwardness even when being watched.

Provided that you have regular coaching sessions with different groups of the cast and for different reasons, the uncoordinated children should not feel that they have been embarrassingly singled out. The choice of the exercises you give them will depend on the individual children. The balance and control exercises might include stretching exercises on one leg to develop a sense of gracefulness and firm control; then balancing two children against one another so that they lean their full weight against each other and see how far they can extend their mutual balance, until they are both standing on one leg, touching by one hand, and leaning at an extreme angle. To develop naturalness in walking and moving, it is often helpful to experiment with different types of imaginary motive force – imagine you are a puppet controlled by strings from above, or by sticks from below; imagine that every movement of your body is derived from your stomach, so that walking and clapping the hands are achieved by an effort that originates at the diaphragm; imagine you are being pulled along by a string attached to your forehead, your chest, your pelvis or your knees; imagine you are pulling or pushing a heavy weight, or being sucked or blown along against your will; imagine you are very heavy or very light or the floor is sticky; and then walk naturally again.

Voice production is another topic that worries many children. Ideally your performance space will be so arranged that your actors do not need to shout in order to be heard. But for some children you may find diction exercises useful – get them to practise any sounds they may find difficult, then to speak their lines over-emphasizing the consonants, then to speak them normally again. Some children may need help with the actual sound production: breathing exercises, and getting them to 'bounce' the sound from the diaphragm, should be helpful; however, it is usually not the volume but the projection of the sense which needs attention. Children who are unaccustomed to speaking in large spaces need to be shown how to pace their words so that they can be distinguished and understood: even a whisper should carry across a hall if the speaker 'thinks' the sense to the back row of the audience.

If children are required to adopt an accent other than their natural one, this too may need tuition. Tapes of the required accents for children to copy may be useful; or if possible think of a television series that uses the accent; then finally your own analysis of the vowel changes involved in each accent will need to be applied to the lines concerned. You may also find it useful to get the cast to improvise using the accent they are trying to assume.

Taking on a character

All the technical points may need to be worked on with some or all of the cast; but far more important is the necessity for you to help every member of the cast to 'feel' and project the emotions of the characters they are playing, and make the whole character real.

Acting involves an identification of the personality of the actor with that of the character, so that the character becomes a real and believable person; and the feelings of the character must be experienced by the actor as the character. To achieve this is extremely difficult even for an adult; for a child, who is probably unsure of his own personality and emotionally inexperienced, it is much harder.

It is to be hoped that the course of your rehearsals, involving improvisation around the script and discussion of the motives and personalities of the characters, will go some way towards helping the cast to assume the personalities of the characters. But you will probably find that some work needs to be done with pairs or small groups, in which the business of identifying the personality of the actor with that of the character can be fully discussed, and the embarrassment of exposing real emotions so that they can be experienced in character can be overcome.

Achieving a reality of complex emotions is particularly difficult. How does a young actor who has led a comparatively sheltered life convey realistically the emotion of a character whose lover has died? You might try telling him to 'Look sad' (overheard at a school I was visiting recently, as an instruction to Orestes arising embarrassed after murdering his mother Clytemnestra) but you would find that this has a pretty grotesque effect – if any. For better (though by no means guaranteed) results, try first relating the moment to any moments of intense emotion which the actor has felt in his own life: how on that occasion did his mouth, his throat, his eyes, his scalp, his stomach, his knees, his breathing feel? And then try – probably through improvisation, or even by the use of mime – to build up the personality of the character through the personality of the actor, so that the actor becomes the character, and becomes able to experience the grief of the character, and to portray it in the scene as if it is a real and actual experience. Not all children will be able to do this – indeed, a good few professional actors can't – but it is a goal to aim at.

If in the end you give up, and decide that this goal cannot be achieved with the actor in question, the one remaining course is to give the child the same instruction that Alfred Hitchcock is said to have given to Ingrid Bergman when she said that she was unable to 'feel' the emotion in one of his scenes: 'Then fake it'.

Two final points to remember throughout the weeks of rehearsal: first, your cast have volunteered to do the play, and are giving up their free time to rehearse it, so the rehearsals must be fun, and you must try never to waste their time. Second, your cast are exposing their selves in a way that does not generally come naturally to adolescents: so they must at all times be confident that you will not let them down by allowing them to make fools of themselves by performing badly in front of the audience in the eventual performances.

9 Backstage

If you are lucky, you have a whole team of staff colleagues, each with a particular backstage skill, and each with the enthusiasm to take full responsibility for his own area, and the willingness to take time and trouble over involving as many pupils as possible in the work.

Unfortunately, you cannot rely on the staff of your particular school having the necessary spread of skills and experience, even if they have the enthusiasm. As the director of the project, you need to have some practical knowledge of all the different types of backstage work, so that you can check that all is being done correctly, you can train your colleagues in aspects of the work, and you can do it yourself if you are unable to find a colleague willing to take the responsibility.

This chapter looks at each of the areas of backstage skill in which you need to have a least a smattering of knowledge. In each area I am assuming that as much as possible of the work is to be done by pupils.

Props

It is hard to generalize on this subject since the requirements of every play are different. As early as possible you need to make a list of all the props that you will require. The easiest way to begin your quest is to pin a notice on the staff-room notice board, to see how many of the required objects can be supplied by teachers. Then make an announcement in school assembly, to see what can be supplied by pupils. Then approach the managers of local stores (especially if they are the fathers of children in your school) to see whether they will be prepared to loan items in return for a programme advertisement. Don't forget to take out adequate insurance on any items of value that are being lent – especially antiques.

Finally, all those abstruse or awkward items which no one has volunteered to supply must be either hired or made. Hiring is generally a last resort: it can be costly, and it usually involves long journeys to collect the items on the day of the dress rehearsal when everyone is too exhausted and busy to cope. As for the making of props, it is up to your inventiveness to devise the simplest ways of making what you need. Teachers of woodwork and metalwork, even if they have been too busy to take the responsibility for all the props, will probably be only too pleased to help with the making of one or two specific objects if you approach them in a suitably flattering vein. Otherwise, it is up to you to do what you can with cardboard boxes, papier mâché, discarded expanded polystyrene packing (which can be picked up at any television or hi-fi store, and can be moulded with a hot knife) and lots of glue, wire and paint. If you use fruit gums for jewellery, don't leave your finished props on a radiator. If you use spray paint, protect the floor, walls, ceilings and children with newspaper. If you are making weapons, don't leave them where bellicose pupils can get at them before the glue is dry.

Finally, once all the props have been assembled, and are ready to be used by the cast, they need to be rigidly supervised by a super-efficient property master (or mistress) who ensures that they are returned to the props table after use – otherwise half of them will get lost in the panic of the dress rehearsal and the first performance.

Costumes

As with props, it is hard to generalize since the requirements of every play are different. Once again, begin with what the actors themselves can produce, or what the school wardrobe (that dusty trunk that the caretakers sit on during their teabreak) has in stock; then see what can be lent by staff, other pupils, and local organizations such as amateur drama clubs; then make the rest. Hire only as a last resort: it seems to be a rule of school drama that the more expensive a hired costume is, the greater the likelihood of its having coffee spilt down it or a child's arm thrust through the wrong holes.

Material for chorus costumes can generally be acquired by appealing throughout the school for discarded curtains and old sheets. Chorus costumes should be simple enough in design for every member of the chorus to make his or her own. Figure 9 shows just how simple a costume can be (it is a design for an all-purpose costume for a chorus of mediaeval peasants). At the opposite extreme, the design and making of really complex

65

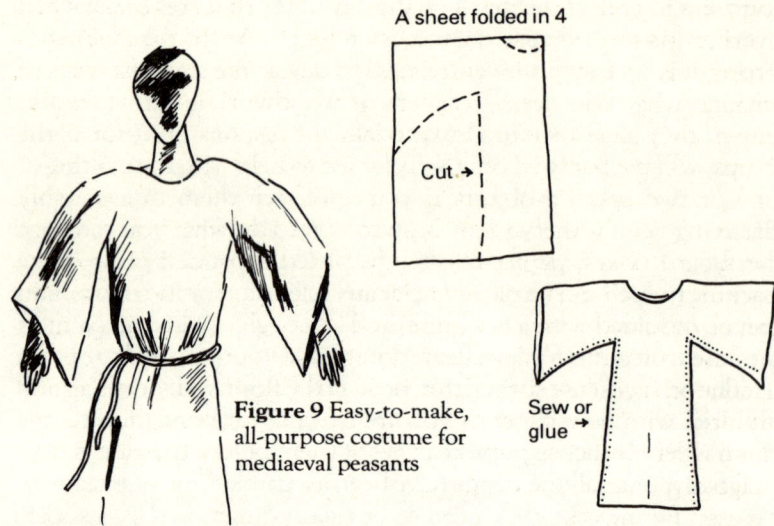

A sheet folded in 4

Cut →

Figure 9 Easy-to-make, all-purpose costume for mediaeval peasants

Sew or glue →

costumes can sometimes be the subject for a CSE project for a fifth-year needlework student.

Scenery

If scenery is being used, it must be totally safe, so that there is no danger of it falling down. The obvious methods of making flats stand up are to fix them with weights and braces (see figure 10:1); to attach hinged buttresses to the back of them (see 10:2); or to hinge them together in twos and threes so that they are free-standing (see 10:3) like a Victorian parlour screen. The first method is the easiest (if you have a stock of weights and braces) but makes scene-changes more complicated; the second allows you to bring a flat on in the middle of a scene with the minimum of fuss; the third method has

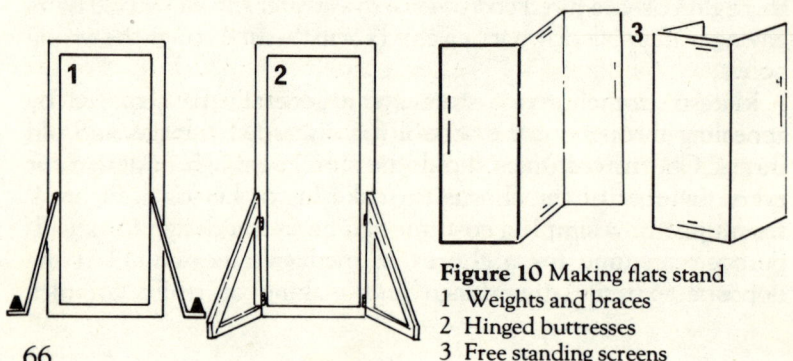

Figure 10 Making flats stand
1 Weights and braces
2 Hinged buttresses
3 Free standing screens

the advantage that both sides of the flats can be painted, and it is a very simple movement to turn them round for a scene-change. As a further alternative, the scenery can be in the form of blocks– triangular or cuboid– which can be turned for an instant scene-change, and can even be strengthened so that actors can stand on them, or fitted with castors and moved around by stage hands concealed inside them.

Whichever method is used, the basic flat is likely to consist of a stout wooden frame, with bracing at the corners, covered with hessian or canvas– or hardboard if a cut-out shape is required. For some sets, the material may need to be covered with a layer of lining paper before the paint is applied; for others, the texture of the hessian or canvas may be an advantage.

The school's woodwork teacher should be able to advise on how to make the frames for the flats. If not, the pattern shown in figure 11 should be simple enough for even the most hamfisted amateur stage-carpenter to cope with.

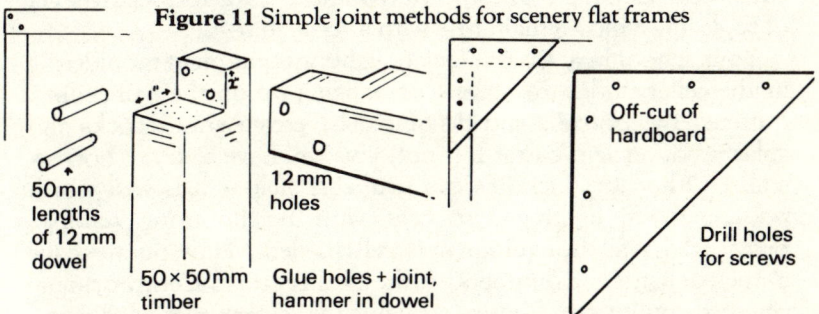

Figure 11 Simple joint methods for scenery flat frames

50 mm lengths of 12 mm dowel

50 × 50 mm timber

12 mm holes

Glue holes + joint, hammer in dowel

Off-cut of hardboard

Drill holes for screws

While building the scenery, watch out for apparently helpful pupil-assistants trying the favourite school-play skivers' trick: a beaming and polite pupil will appear at your elbow just before the end of a lesson and ask if he can fetch anything for you. If you thoughtlessly send him on an errand – say to get some more nails from the woodwork room – you will find that the errand takes him precisely 55 minutes, and he reappears just before the end of the next lesson in the hope of repeating the exercise. In the intervening time he will have explained to whichever of your colleagues should be teaching him that he cannot attend their lessons because you have asked him to help build scenery for the school play; and then, assuming that you will be far to preoccupied to remember how long he has been gone, he will have disappeared for who-knows-what debauchery behind the bicycle sheds.

The painting of the scenery can be a project for a whole team of pupils: arm each with a brush and some paint, mark out the areas that are to be covered with each colour, and you will find the basic background complete within a short space of time (the floor will also be daubed in an artistic array of colours unless you have taken suitable precautions). The shading and detail can then be added by whoever has the requisite artistic talent.

Lighting

Lighting is comparatively simple if you have the right equipment; but, being electrical, it is potentially dangerous, and I recommend that even if you have no member of staff with skill and experience in this field, you ensure that your lighting team is always accompanied by an adult. All children involved should be made aware of the reasons for earthing and fusing, and the dangers of worn wiring, defective plugs and sockets, and trying to save time by taking short cuts. I once came across a technically-minded sixth-former in the act of replacing a blown main fuse with a six-inch nail...

Your school may have a stock of lighting equipment mouldering in the cellar under the stage – or hanging up on the hall ceiling, buffeted by footballs and decorated by errant shuttlecocks and splashes of ancient custard. If not, you will have to try to borrow some. Other local schools can probably help – it is well worth pooling your lighting resources with neighbouring schools, provided that all the equipment is well labelled. Many counties have a stock of lights and dimmers – in the local Teachers' Centre or some obscure county warehouse – available for schools that need them. The local amateur drama society may be able to lend you equipment. Or, as a last resort, you may have to hire. But before doing this, it is always worth consulting your county drama adviser, who will know whether and where any equipment is available within the county.

Long before you need to think about setting up your lights, check over all the equipment for safety and efficiency. Are all the bulbs screwed in tight? Are all the plugs correctly wired? Does every light have an earth wire firmly attached to its metal casing? Are any of the connecting wires starting to look worn? Do all your hanging lights have safety chains? Have you a sufficient stock of spare bulbs and fuses?

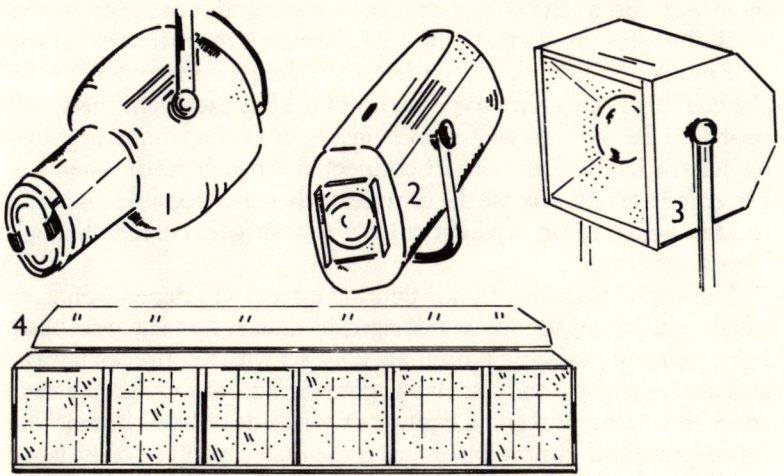

Figure 12 1 Spotlight; 2 Fresnel spot; 3 Floodlight; 4 Floodlight batten

You are likely to encounter three basic types of light: (figure 12) the spot, the flood, and the fresnel spot. The spotlight produces a directable hard-edged beam of light, which can be focused to make it as wide or narrow as you require. The floodlight produces a general wash of light over a wide area in front of it. Floodlights are sometimes cased together in rows to form battens, which when equipped with suitable coloured gels give you the facility of changing the general colour of your acting area. Fresnel spotlights have specially moulded lenses to diffuse the light, producing a directional but soft-edged beam. (No two lighting technicians seem to agree on the pronunciation of 'fresnel'.)

The lights can either be hung from bars on the ceiling (in which case both the bars and the individual lights need safety chains), or they can be fixed to scaffolding towers, or they can be on stands on the floor. Using lights upside down will decrease the life of the bulbs, which are extremely expensive. For the same reason, try to avoid moving lights about when they are still warm from use.

The lights are connected by cables to your control panel. If the cables are too long they should not be used while in a tight coil, but should be spread out, since a live coil will overheat. Cables should not be placed where the cast or audience can trip over them or small children can play with them.

Your control panel should, with luck, include a number of dimmers, with which you can control the intensity of the lights. The dimmers will either be heavy mechanical ones, consisting of a coil of wire round a slate core, or more modern and more economical small thyrister dimmers. Do not be alarmed if the mechanical type of dimmer gets hot when your lights are dim: it is meant to. (Do be alarmed if smoke starts to pour out of it.) For each light there will probably be a three-way switch giving you the opportunity of having the light full on, off, or connected through the dimmer. It is better for the bulbs to use the dimmers whenever possible, since the sudden switching on of a light sends a huge surge of current through your system.

The sophistication of your lighting effects will depend on how much equipment you have managed to amass. For a general basic light, you will probably illuminate your set with a couple of floods, and use spotlights and fresnels to light your actors. Divide the acting space into areas, and aim a light from each side onto each area. The more lights and dimmers you have, the easier it will be to isolate a particular part of the acting area, or change the colour of the light, for specific scenes.

Figure 13 shows an extremely simple lighting set-up using two floods and four spots. With this arrangement you can light the entire stage (by using all six lights); or you can isolate one part of the stage (by using just lights 3 and 6) or the other (just lights 4 and 5); or

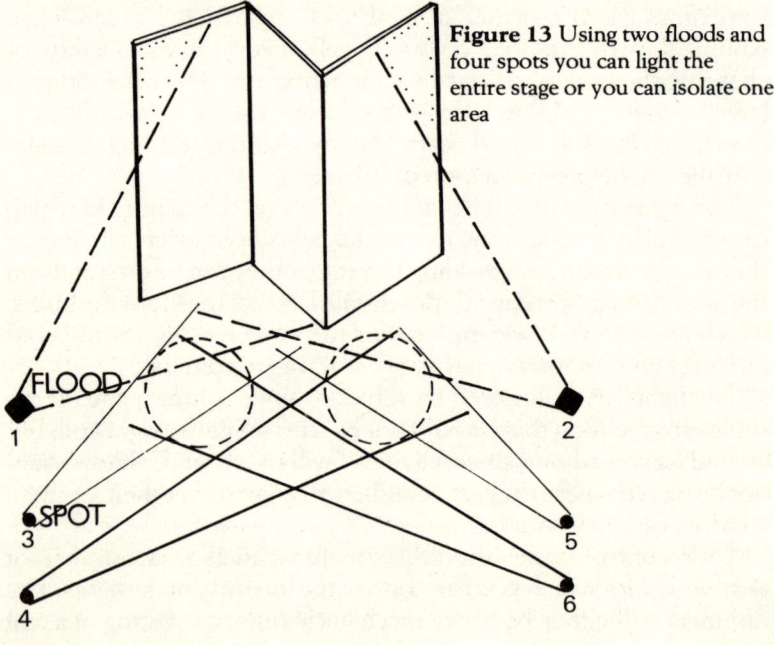

Figure 13 Using two floods and four spots you can light the entire stage or you can isolate one area

you can produce a stark, shadowy effect across the stage (by using 3 and 4 only, or 5 and 6 only); or you can silhouette your actors against the set (by using only lights 1 and 2). If each of your lights contains a different coloured gel you can further vary the mood.

For a larger acting space, this simple basic plan can be multiplied as often as you like, so that you may be working with ten or 15 areas, each with a light from each side focused onto it. If you are acting in the round, each area may need three or four lights to illuminate it from all directions.

For further more sophisticated effects you will need to hire or borrow specialist equipment. A follow-spot is a mobile spotlight on a stand, the beam of which can be moved around to follow a moving actor or create a searchlight effect. A strobe light is one that flashes on and off many times per second to create a jerky 'silent movie' impression (but follow the instructions carefully, as certain fast flashing-speeds at close quarters are thought to be capable of inducing epilepsy). An ultra-violet light will show up only those items that are specially painted or treated. An effects-wheel is a rotating device which goes in front of a light, changing the effect of the beam according to a set programme (effects-wheels are very popular in discos for producing varying coloured patterns; other types can create impressions of fire, passing clouds, etc). It is also possible to project colour transparencies onto part of the set – but remember that most projectors contain irritatingly noisy fans.

Whoever controls the lights at your eventual performances will need a script clearly marked with numbered cues, a team of children to operate the dimmers, and a sense of humour for when fuses start blowing in the middle of a show.

Make-up

There are two reasons why an actor might wear stage make-up: to emphasize his features so that his facial expressions can be seen clearly from a distance, or under very powerful lights; or to add age or 'character' to his features. The first reason is unlikely to be applicable in the case of a school play: the distances will probably not be so great, nor the lights so powerful, as to render the wearing of make-up necessary. Indeed, wearing make-up is often a positive mistake, as unless it is extremely subtle it will show up as make-up, and destroy the impression of naturalness that 'straight' make-up is intended to convey. For most of your performers the only make-up that might be necessary is a little eye emphasis: but this should be so

71

subtle that even the front row of the audience can scarcely detect it as make-up. Most girls will be familiar with the principles of eye make-up: your main task is to restrain them from going wild with their most lurid eye-shadow in the excitement of the moment. The eye in figure 14 shows the sort of emphasis that might be useful for a boy's eyes. The lines should be painted on with a small brush or an orange stick; the colour used will range from black for a black-haired actor to light brown for a blond actor.

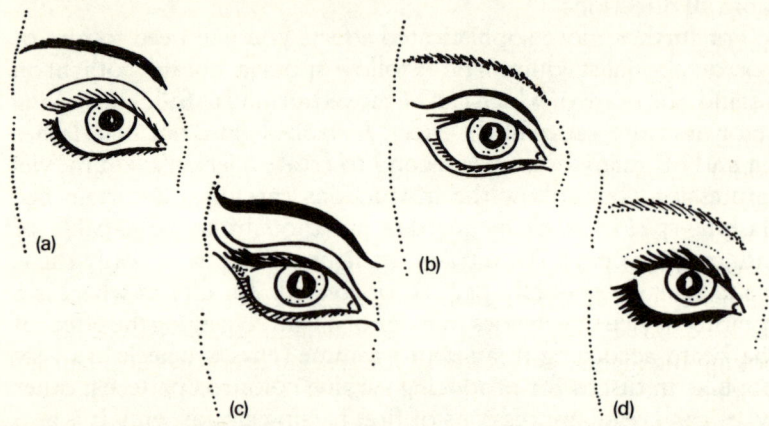

Figure 14 Eye make up
(a) Simple eye line. Lightly mascared lashes and lightly pencilled eyebrows
(b) 'The New Alien'. Emphasis with deep-coloured pencils and shadow
(c) 'The Extended Alien'. Liberal use of pencil and mascara. An exotically graphic approach
(d) Eye emphasis only. False lashes and heavy use of mascara

The second reason for wearing make-up – the adding of age or character to a young face – may be more necessary in your play, as face make-up can sometimes help a young actor to feel old. But make-up is no substitute for acting technique: and before smothering the faces of your 'character' actors with layers of greasepaint, it is worth considering whether a better performance might not be achieved by using no make-up at all – ie by frankly admitting to the audience that this is a young actor pretending to be old, and allowing him to use his walk, his movements, his voice and his facial expressions to suggest his age.

If, however, you do decide to use character make-up, it is valuable to teach the actors how to apply their own make-up rather than getting a teacher to do it all, so that the actor can wrinkle by wrinkle assume the character he is going to play, and he can see as he makes himself up how his facial expressions are looking.

72

The aim of character make-up is to suggest hollows and wrinkles by contrasting them with highlights. For old age, lower cheeks and eye sockets will be hollowed (ie darkened) and contrasted with nose-ridges and cheek-bones, which will be highlighted. Wrinkles can be painted into all the places where the young actor finds wrinkles when he screws up his face; and further aging can be gained by painting in bags under the eyes. To look like a wrinkle, each dark line needs to have a highlight beside it – study the way the light falls on an actual old person's face. Harsh lines on the cheeks and round the mouth tend to produce a more severe expression, while 'crow's feet' round the eyes suggest more jollity or benevolence. The colours to be used will depend on the natural colouring of the actor's hair and complexion, and whether the characters are basically indoor or outdoor people. The basic foundation will probably be Leichner no. 5 ('Ivory') mixed with no. 9 ('Brick Red') or no. 8 ('Golden Tan'), or possibly a touch of no. 4½ ('Brownish Tan') or no. 6½ ('Light Olive'), in varying degrees to make the hollows and highlights. Lines and wrinkles can be painted on with Lake, Brown, Black or Dark Grey. White can produce particularly unhealthy-looking highlights, and is useful for greying eyebrows and hair at temples. The make-up generally needs to be powdered after application to prevent it from running or smudging.

In all use of make-up it is better to be subtle than blatant. It is far more effective for young actors to have very little make-up, and have to rely on their acting technique to suggest character, than to have too much make-up, and look more like clowns than characters. Excessive character make-up can also ruin an actor's naturally varying facial expressions – if he has a particular expression painted onto his face, the effect when he laughs might be grotesque.

Non-realistic make-up, on the other hand, can be as blatant as you like, and is very effective for choruses. A chorus of policemen might all be sporting black walrus moustaches. A chorus of bridesmaids might all have white faces with round red cheeks, like wooden dolls. A chorus of pirates might all have their right eyes blackened and huge scars on their left cheeks. A group of impersonal guards can be transformed into something very sinister by giving them white faces with black features painted on in harsh straight lines.

For specific make-up patterns for clowns, Red Indians, negroes, or any extreme type of characterization, consult Messrs Leichner for advice – but be aware that the make-up charts they publish are designed to make every feature stand out at a distance of a hundred yards.

Some children may find that greasepaint reacts unpleasantly with their skins: for these the water-based Pancake range of make-ups may be preferable as a foundation. Greasepaint can be removed by softening it with any kind of grease or face cream, wiping it off with a tissue, and then washing thoroughly with soap and water.

Sound

I recommend that you keep sound effects live whenever possible, since there are so many things that can (and do) go wrong with a tape-recorder. Few dramatic moments can be more ludicrous than a series of taped sound effects that get out of synchronization with the action, and once the wrong sound starts, the inevitability is awful; whereas with a group of children operating noise-making gadgets, any sort of instant correction can be made. Moreover, standing backstage making noises of storms and explosions and breaking crockery is much more fun than operating tape recorders.

However, if you decide that a tape is necessary then you must find a foolproof way of marking the tape so that you have split-second control of your cueing. The most efficient method is to splice sections of coloured leader tape into your sound tape, and to use these in conjunction with careful observation of the numbers on the rev counter on your tape deck. Trying to operate a sound tape on cassette never really works, since it is impossible to have sufficiently precise control of exact moments on the tape.

Stage management

The stage manager is completely responsible for the smooth running of the dress rehearsal and the performances. His responsibility is total: so he needs to be involved in the rehearsals from an early point, and to know the play extremely well. During the performance he may well have a hundred people under his command – actors, chorus, stage crew, lighting team, sound team, props supervisers, callboys, etc; so he must be totally calm, efficient and confident in management, commanding everyone's respect, and able to delegate wherever necessary. In order to do his job properly, he must know what everyone should be doing at every moment during the show: and so he must be fully involved in the production from the start. His tasks include ensuring that everyone

74

connected with the show has done his or her job by the time of the dress rehearsal; checking that cast and helpers arrive on time for the performances; ensuring that every member of the cast appears on stage on cue; controlling all the actors backstage, making sure they keep out of the way, are ready to enter, and don't make a noise backstage; passing on all cues to the lighting and sound operators during the performance; organizing the scene-changes; clearing up after each performance so that everything is ready for the next day; and generally co-ordinating every aspect of the running of the performance.

Nine times out of ten he turns out to be you. But if you can find a colleague – or possibly even a senior pupil – whom you can rely upon totally to the extent of trusting him or her with the task of stage management, then you are a lucky director; and the show will probably run that much more smoothly because your own panicking self is not directly involved in the running of the performance.

10 *Publicity*

If you have taken the last few chapters to heart, there are now a few hundred children working hard to make your production an artistic success. It would be a sad deflation of all this massed enthusiasm if you were to end up performing to rows of empty chairs. However, the lure of the television and the appeal of apathy are powerful enemies to live theatre, and you must mount a strong – and early – publicity campaign, in order to ensure that you play to a capacity house at every performance.

If you are hoping to be allowed by your Head Teacher to put on another play next year, full houses are also important because you want to cover all your costs. In fact, you should be able to make a profit, since the main financial outlay for any professional theatre company – actors' wages – is not applicable to your production. (If you do make a profit, do your utmost to ensure that it goes into a special fund for drama equipment, and not into the School Fund.)

But contemplation of how to spend your profits is arrant chicken-counting at this stage. First, deal with your publicity. Your audience can be thought of as dividing themselves into four separate areas, each of which requires a different type of approach: children in the school; parents and friends of children in the school; the general public; and special concessions to certain groups.

Publicity within the school

The most effective way of getting every child in the school to attend the performances is to have every child involved in some way in the work of the production. In most schools this is an unattainable ideal, so you will need to mount a powerful campaign in the school, starting perhaps a month before the opening performance. Your campaign probably begins with you addressing the school at a morning assembly – or in smaller groups at house or year assemblies.

The whole school should already be familiar with the theme of the play: but a few reminders may be useful. Then you will need to explain how many thousand tickets you hope to sell, how when and where they will be available, and how every pupil can help in the sales and publicity.

For the month leading up to the performance, every child must know where tickets can be bought – otherwise on the day when he remembers to bring the money it may well get spent on chips or cigarettes. How you organize the availability of tickets will depend on the structure of your school. You might operate a box office, staffed by a rota of responsible pupils, at a certain place every lunch hour; or you might collect orders from each class tutor and supply the tickets by paper-clipping them to the registers; or you might have a team of volunteers from your own tutor group who between them visit every class during registration; or you might do your selling through the English department, so that children know that tickets can be purchased at the beginning of every English lesson. The important thing is that the pupils are reminded regularly – preferably every day – that the tickets are easily available.

Nearer the time of the performance – perhaps a week in advance – some larger gimmick might be necessary to encourage the interest of those pupils who have still not purchased tickets. One particularly effective idea is to stage a short excerpt from your play as a sort of 'trailer' at a full school assembly. The excerpt need be no more than a couple of minutes long, and you can discuss with your cast which scene they think might appeal most to the audience; it should preferably be something strongly visual, and it should end at a critical point – a technique you can usefully borrow from the writers of those children's comics who contrive every week to leave the hero enmeshed in the coils of a six-headed space serpent or the heroine in the clutches of a 16-stone rapist: 'To find out what happens next, come and see the play…' To take a section of the play in which the actors feel fairly confident and expose it to an audience a week or so before the first performance is a useful exercise for your cast anyway, since it gives them a brief taste of the effects of stage nerves, which they can analyze with a view to increasing their confidence for the actual performances.

Parents, friends and neighbours

Fairly early in your publicity campaign a letter needs to go out to the parents of all the pupils in the school, giving full details of the play and inviting them to buy tickets. Letters sent to parents via their offspring do not always reach home – they often remain in anorak pockets for weeks, or worse still end up as pastel-coloured aeroplanes in gardens adjoining the roads leading to the school – but a certain proportion will find their way home, and this is probably the best you can do. (If the timing is on your side, the best way of getting letters home is to stick them in the envelopes with the school reports: only those pupils who are extremely adept at forging their parents' signatures will fail to deliver these).

Earlier still in the course of the production, you will have arranged for a poster to be designed. You may have a particularly artistic pupil to whom this task can be assigned; alternatively you can raise interest generally by making the design of the poster a competition throughout the school. The basic principles of poster design – legibility and 'noticeability' – can be expounded by yourself or your colleagues in the art department, and the wording for the poster given to all entrants. All entries can be used as in-school advertising, and then gathered together as a foyer display for the nights of the performances; and the best two can be turned into an A4 duplicated handbill and a full-size silk-screen or lino-cut poster, and mass-produced. The choice of a prize will depend on how much incentive you deem necessary: if you can get enough entries with the offer of a bar of chocolate it may not be necessary to offer a £5 book token. But generally you will find it money well spent to make your prize something at least £5 in value, so that pupils are encouraged to take time and trouble over the designs they submit.

Once you have mass-produced your handbills and posters, you need to ensure that every shop, public building and notice board in the catchment area of your school is displaying a poster. The distribution of these should be the responsibility of every child in the school; but in practice you will find it easiest to appoint a pair of volunteers to take responsibility for each road or area, so that a general cover of the district is achieved with as little wastage as possible.

Your classroom sales campaign should stress that it is important for children not only to buy tickets themselves, but also to sell them to their parents, their aunts and cousins and grandparents, and all their neighbours. If it can be administered simply, it may be worth instituting a sale-or-return system for children willing to sell tickets to neighbours and relations: but this needs to be done in good time, so that when you are within a week of the first performance you know exactly how many tickets are still unsold.

The General Public

Many school plays are never really advertised to the general public. This is a policy decision that needs to be made in conjunction with your Head Teacher; but it seems to me that a major opportunity is being missed if you do not encourage the general public to come and see your play. Not only do the public represent a valuable source of revenue; but all sorts of benefits accrue – both to the status of the school within the community, and to the status of yourself as a teacher of drama within the school – if your school can gain a wide and generally-acknowledged reputation as a local cultural centre where plays of a high standard can regularly be seen.

The extensive distribution of posters will help to remind the public about your play; but to attract their initial attention, you need to do something bigger and more striking.

If you can, you should aim to get a photograph – and preferably a story as well – onto the front page of your local newspaper on all of the last four weeks before the performance. A certain amount of tactics are required to achieve this. Most local newspaper offices are staffed either by a few extremely overworked journalists, or by a large number of underworked but inexperienced 'juniors'. In either case, they will greatly appreciate it if you write your own articles and submit them, neatly typed, rather than require a member of their staff to do some work. Do not be bashful: many a time I have known local papers report 'yet another triumph for Peter Griffith, the play's highly talented and experienced director' – and only I and the sub-editors know who wrote the article.

The situation with photographs is rather different: if the paper has a photographer or two on the staff, the editor will prefer not to print photos submitted by you, since to do so would be to risk angering the NUJ and also to deprive his paper of revenue from the sale of additional prints. If the paper has no staff photographer but relies on a local studio, it might be worthwhile submitting a few large prints: and you may find that you stand the best chance of getting one published if a friend – or yourself in disguise – poses as a professional photographer and sells it to the editor at his standard rate, rather than you simply giving it to him and asking him to print it as a favour.

But it is probably less trouble, and brings a greater chance of the photo being printed, if you rely on the paper's regular photographer. To get a subject photographed for the paper, it must include at least ten children. However uninspired the photograph, if it contains ten children that means ten sets of parents and twenty sets of grandparents who will buy additional copies of the paper that week and order additional prints from the photographer. That is how local photo-journalists think: so your task is to find a topic each week that gives an excuse for a photo of ten or more children. If you can include 20 children, you have doubled your chances of inclusion in the paper, even if you have halved the artistic possibilities of the picture.

The same goes for mentions of children's names in your article: if you can conclude your piece with a list of 50 children involved in the aspect of the show you are writing about, you are increasing fiftyfold the chances of the article being published. As well as this, you want the coverage of your play to be on the front page each week: so you always have to provide a good gimmick or 'intro' to your press release. The first sentence is the most important: it must be short, clear and astonishing. Suitable subjects for 'pre-pieces' (articles printed in advance of the first performance) might include features on any unusual aspect of the props (eg photo of children carrying life-size dummies through the streets, having borrowed them from a local department store for the bridal store scene in *West Side Story*) or the scenery (eg children manoeuvring the car that is to be used in the 'Greased Lightning' scene in *Grease*) or the costumes (any particularly spectacular dresses – especially if designed or worn by a photogenic pupil) or the music (eg taking delivery of the harpsichord for *Tom Jones*) or the production itself (rehearsal photos of any spectacular fights or dance routines). In every case, the 'intro' to your article needs to highlight some unusual (or better still extraordinary or utterly bizarre) aspect of the preparations for your play. Remember that the editor of your local paper is not interested in providing a balanced or even a true account of your play, but in publishing articles that will help to sell newspapers. Once you have attracted the editor's favour and the reader's attention by your 'intro', you need to find any available excuse for including the full details of the times, dates, and prices of your performances, and where tickets can be purchased, before closing with mentions of as many children's names as can reasonably be fitted in.

As well as the 'pre-pieces', a complimentary review of your production is good for cast morale, and can help to sell the last few tickets if it is published before the end of the show's run. In the event of a reporter being sent along to the first performance, ensure that he or she is let in free and provided with free drinks or coffee and a free programme with difficult names underlined or rewritten in block capitals. (The reference to drinks is particularly important if you get an experienced journalist along: I know a number of experienced journalists who only work at their best when in an alcoholic stupor, and tend to write somewhat jaded reviews if they have to give up an evening to see a show and no one buys them a drink.) If no reporter is sent, hand in your own totally complimentary review – including modest quotations from yourself to the effect that it was really the kids that made the show – as soon as the news office opens on the following morning.

The technique for getting yourself onto local radio or television is similar to that employed for newspapers, except that in these cases you are only likely to be featured once, so you need to choose your moment and your subject carefully, and try to lure the media in with the most unusual and bizarre facet that your production offers; it might be some aspect of the rehearsal or preparation, or it might be some unusual or controversial scene from the play. Paradoxically, a spot of bad publicity can often be very helpful. If an antiquated local councillor or school governor complains that the play contains language or concepts that he considers unsuitable for children – or better still that he thinks the whole play a waste of time – this gives you the cue to produce a full-scale reply explaining the whole basis of school drama and demonstrating the degree of involvement and sophistication shown by your pupils, which will not only make the complainer look silly but will also be excellent publicity for the play. (In extreme cases it may be worth stirring up this sort of publicity by writing a letter of complaint to your local paper under a pseudonym.)

As well as getting a full feature on local radio and television, you need to try to get a mention on the 'What's On' programmes put out by the media. They like to have the material for these as early as possible – preferably several weeks in advance.

If you want to sell tickets to the general public, you need to persuade some central shop or office to act as your box office. In any school you will have a number of pupils whose parents own or manage shops: so if possible try to cajole one of these into selling the tickets. If you cannot get a friendly shop to oblige, then you may have to pay a commission to a travel agent to do the job; but whoever does the selling, make sure you approach them early enough to include their name on the posters.

Another simple and useful publicity method is to duplicate slips of paper advertising the play (you can get four or five from each A4 sheet) and persuade local newsagents to distribute these with the local papers. Occasionally newsagents make a small charge for this: but they will usually do it free – especially when you point out that the actual work will be done by the delivery boys and girls, who are almost certainly pupils of yours.

If you really want to make an impact on your area, there are various more extreme gimmicks that can be used. One idea is a parade through your local town or towns of members of your cast in costume, carrying banners and giving our handbills, and possibly stopping wherever there is room to perform brief excerpts or rehearsed jingles. To do this you need to check with the local police in advance: they will seldom raise any objection provided that you promise not to obstruct the roadway or pavements – indeed they may well offer helpful advice as to a suitable route for your procession. The local council may get worried because they think you are collecting money; once they discover that you aren't they should leave you alone.

Another way of making an impact on a town is to hang a banner across one of the main streets. You will need to apply to your local council for permission at least four months in advance – preferably six or eight or ten months – so that they have plenty of time to pass the subject from committee to committee and compose suitable dockets and memos about it. If they finally agree, you will need to find two buildings opposite one another whose owners are willing to let you hang the banner from their windows, in such a way that the banner will be above the level of double-decker buses. Your local boy scouts or army cadets can probably lend you the ropes you will need, and possibly also the strong canvas onto which your message will be written. Cut-out felt letters are probably the most weatherproof. Any structural sewing on your canvas – such as the hems through which the ropes pass – must be extremely strong, as the banner is going to be subject to very great wind pressure. When you erect the banner, remember to check with the police first as the traffic may need to be stopped. To get the banner into position, simply drop a length of string out of the window each side of the road; attach your ropes to the strings; and then pull the banner up. You will find that, unless you restrain them, your pupils will take a fiendish delight in risking their lives perching on outside window-ledges four storeys up. If any such risks have to be taken, they must be taken by members of staff – preferably teachers with mountaineering experience who are accustomed to heights and can advise on safety precautions; or, failing that, you...

Special Concessions

Unless things have gone very wrong, your last night will be a sell-out quite early on: it is traditionally the night when the families of the cast attend the performance. But you may find that not so many people want to come to the first performance. So it may be worth offering seats at reduced prices to local organizations for the first performance. And if this idea proves popular, you might think of arranging an additional early performance – a sort of extra dress rehearsal. Parties from other local schools can be invited to this – either at a reduced cost, or free by reciprocal arrangement. And local old people's homes or clubs, and homes for the mentally or physically handicapped, may similarly be pleased to bring parties at a reduced rate. If transport is a problem, local charitable organizations like the Lions Club or the Round Table may be willing to pay for coaches or specialized ambulances to bring elderly or handicapped people in.

One word of warning to pass on to your cast: severely physically handicapped people may not be able to show their appreciation by applause – an obvious point, but the silence at the end of the show can be unnerving to inexperienced actors if they are not prepared for it.

Special performances to audiences from local homes and institutions will not only provide a full house of strangers for the nerve-wracking first performance, but can also do a great deal of good for the elderly and the handicapped, and hence for the school's standing in the community. If as well as giving them a performance you can get the cast to talk to the audience afterwards, and can get other pupils to serve tea to them, then further good can be done. I have frequently found that the most disruptive and aggressive pupils are totally charming and responsible when dealing with elderly or handicapped people from their community; and many children are quite unaware of the plight of people less fortunate than themselves; while old and handicapped people, who often get little opportunity to talk to young people from the community outside their institutions, are quite delighted to be able to build and maintain links with local schools.

11 *Finance*

In the present political and economic climate, with capitation allowances being cut on all sides, Parent Teacher Associations having to take over responsibility for raising money to buy essentials like exercise-books because schools can no longer afford them, and thousands of teachers out of work because Local Education Authorities cannot afford to employ them, it will be difficult to persuade even the most sympathetic Head Teacher that the school play is so essential a part of school life that the spending of large amounts of money on it can be justified. Schools seem to be approaching a situation where the spending of money on anything – justifiable or not – will be out of the question, as there will be no money to spend. Therefore the school play needs financially to stand on its own feet, just like any other amateur or professional theatrical organization.

So your budget must be planned very carefully; and you need to think hard about how money can be saved, and how money can be raised. At the time of writing inflation is running at 22 per cent; so there is little point in my mentioning actual figures in this chapter, since by the date of publication they would already be out of date.

The following items may need to be allowed for in your budget:

Royalties

Copies of the script

Costumes –
hired
bought
material
cotton, zips, trimmings, etc

Scenery –
timber
hardboard
canvas or hessian

paint and brushes
nails, screws, hinges, etc

Props –
hired
bought
made

Lighting –
hire of equipment
cables, plugs, adaptors, etc
spare bulbs
electricity

Sound –
tapes
hire of equipment
cables, plugs, adaptors, etc
hire of musical instruments
fees to professional musicians

Insurance –
to cover all borrowed and hired items

Transport –
for collecting and returning hired and borrowed items
for getting people to and from rehearsals and performances

Make-up

Publicity –
posters
handbills
slips for newsagents
additional gimmicks (street banners, etc)
photographs

Programmes and tickets –
paper
printing

Coffee, sugar, milk for the interval

Hire of hall (if playing outside school)

Miscellaneous (stamps; phone calls; cans of beer for caretakers; dry cleaning of hired costume that had coffee spilt down it; tranquillizers to control your panic during final week of rehearsals; etc, etc.)

Saving money

Obviously every play has different requirements, and every area offers different possibilities. The following ideas for skimping, saving and scrounging are all based on my own experience: and you should be able to contribute many more ideas. (If you come up with any really superb ones please let me know by writing to me c/o Batsford Academic and Educational Limited, 4 Fitzhardinge Street, London, W1H 0AH).

If there is an industrial estate near you, take a look at the piles of rubbish near the factory gates. Many factories regularly throw out items which can be used for building scenery. In particular look for firms which use fork lift trucks: every time goods are delivered by this method, the boxes or crates need to be separated by wooden pallets to allow the forks to get under them. These pallets are often thrown out or burnt after a delivery has been made; and although they are made of cheap splintery wood, the pallets can be useful sources of timber for scenery.

If you decide that you cannot afford canvas or hessian to cover your flats, then cardboard will do. It's not so tough or so durable, but it's free. Giant cardboard boxes can be picked up from shops selling televisions, fridges, etc, or from factories that receive consignments of car spares or anything delicate and large.

Firms dealing with heavy-duty cable often have large wooden cable-drums to dispose of. These may be as much as five feet in diameter, and make ideal movable rostrum blocks when placed on their sides.

Copies of scripts can often be acquired by borrowing them from another school that has recently presented the same play. And don't forget to attend all local jumble sales – you never know what you might pick up in the way of costumes and props.

Many people have old half-used tins of paint quietly mouldering in their garages and garden sheds. An appeal throughout the school might well bring you large amounts of free paint: and even if the colours aren't ideal for your play, they will give you a good start. Similarly, pupils might be able to persuade their parents to part with old torn sheets and curtains that could be used as material for costumes.

Paper manufacturers often give away 'seconds' – paper that is not quite up to the standard required by their customers – to their employees. They may be persuaded to donate paper for posters and programmes for your play – especially if some of their employees have children in your school.

For supplies of unusual materials, try the advertisements in hobby and interest magazines – for example, if you need a large area of plastic sheeting, think who might regularly use such a commodity: a gardener, perhaps. So look at the advertisements in gardening magazines for cheap offers.

Parents of your pupils, husbands and wives of your staff colleagues,and school governors, may all be useful contacts. Find out whether any of them owns an antique shop and might be willing to lend furniture; or owns a hardware store and might be prepared to give discount on screws and nails; or runs a building firm and might lend you scaffolding; or works in a drapery store and might be able to acquire extra-cheap remnants of material; or owns a bank...

Even if they are not controlled by specific contacts of yours, local firms and stores may well be willing to help out with loan of props, or the supply of small items – a jar of coffee, a pot of paint, a few reels of cotton – in return for a mention in the programme. This is particularly likely if the shop is new to the area, or its owner is seeking election to the local council or has some other specific reason for wishing to cultivate public goodwill.

Printing of posters, handbills and programmes can probably be done within the school. If your school does not possess the duplicating machines you need – or if it does possess them but there is a three-week waiting list for their use – then your local Teachers' Centre (if it still exists following the government's latest cuts in education expenditure) or the Resources Centre of your local Technical College, Polytechnic or University can probably help.

Before hiring anything, contact your County Drama Adviser (assuming that he, too, still exists after the aforementioned spending cuts) to find out if he knows where it can be borrowed for free.

Finally, remember throughout that it's not just you trying to scrounge all the items you need for your play: every pupil in the school can help. However bizarre your requirements, if several hundred people are looking for it there's a chance that someone will be able to locate whatever you need.

Raising money

However successful your scrounging technique, there will remain a number of items on your budget which cannot be avoided.

You hope that your box office takings will account for at least some of these: but – especially if this is your first production in the area – it is better not to set your sights too high. Many people who would think nothing of paying £1.50 to go to a cinema or £5 to go to a football match would be aghast at the idea of paying out 75p to see a play. So before you can start to charge even remotely realistic prices for your tickets, you must have built up a solid local reputation over the course of several outstanding productions. To begin with, it is preferable to have a capacity audience who have all paid a small amount than a three-quarters empty house of moneyed connoisseurs.

Even if you feel that you can rely on good box office takings (a large cast will at least guarantee a large audience of parents provided that your show does not clash with a major football match), unfortunately most of your bills will have to be paid in advance of the performances. So you need a supply of money in advance which – unless it is left over from the profits of your previous production – must be raised. You may feel that as a highly trained professional teacher it is not your job to spend your time organizing jumble sales and begging for money in order to subsidize your work in school; you would be right: but in a society where even skilled surgeons have to devote much of their energy to fund-raising in order to support their research, you cannot afford to have principles if you wish to do your job effectively.

Raising money for a school play is not easy; but it is easier than raising money for almost anything else, because you have such a vast and enthusiastic manpower at your disposal. But before turning to the standard non-dramatic forms of fund-raising as practised by every charity committee in the country (coffee mornings, jumble sales, sponsored walks, etc) consider the various ways of raising money through your production. Four pages of advertisements in your programme could easily raise £50 for a start. You are unlikely to have much difficulty in selling advertising space to local shops: but if you find few takers, make for shops owned or managed by parents of children in the school, or shops dealing in goods that might appeal to teenagers – sports shops, sweet shops, fashion boutiques – and point out just how many programmes you are proposing to print, and how wide a cross-section of the local community will receive them.

If your production is particularly ambitious, or depends for its dramatic effect upon a particularly ambitious prop, it may be worth approaching local firms for sponsorship. In the present economic situation you are unlikely to be successful: but it is worth a try. In asking for sponsorship, the main point to remember is to be totally specific: explain to the firm exactly how much money you want, for what specific tangible purpose, and precisely how you can benefit them in return by getting their name onto the programme, onto the front page of the local paper, and even onto the stage if practicable.

Of the standard fund-raising procedures, the easiest to organize is the disco. Find out where a disco can be hired cheaply (if none of your pupils has a brother or friend that runs one, then ask the nearest youth leader for advice); book a suitable hall (it is better not to hold the event in school, where you run the risk of inflaming the Head Teacher and putting off a number of your pupils); get your cast, or your pupil fund-raising committee if you have one, to sell the tickets among their friends; and rake in the money. You will need to be firm as to the limitations you impose upon those eligible to buy tickets: keep it strictly within a certain age range, and restrict it to your own school, or two or three local schools. Make sure that a teacher from every school involved is present at the event, so that every child there is known to at least one adult; but make sure that any disciplining that may be necessary is done (gently and tactfully!) by your pupils, who are the organizers of the event, and not by the adults, who are there merely to help and supervise. You will need to buy whatever soft drinks you propose to sell, plastic cups, and crisps; hot dogs also go down well if you or some of your pupils feel energetic enough to cook and sell them. Try to arrange for your local youth club to buy in any provisions you may have left over at the end – that way you can order plenty without fear of wastage (the youth club may also have a cash-and-carry card which will enable you to get the provisions more cheaply). Any youth leader will give you specific advice on running discos in your area. From my own experience I would advise that, since it is at least partly a school event, you insist on no smoking and no alcohol within the hall; but that you do not cause unnecessary friction by seeking out those who wish to smoke outside the hall and out of your sight. Otherwise, let your pupils do all the organizing of the event, while you merely supervise benignly and stand on call in case anything should go wrong.

Jumble sales can raise even more money than discos: but they involve much more hard work. As before, your pupils will do most of this work. If you duplicate 1000 slips advertising the sale and asking people to donate jumble, it won't take long for 50 of your pupils to distribute these to 1000 houses. And you can catch another large market even more quickly simply by announcing the event in a school assembly. For a week leading up to the sale, you need to have some storage space – a garage or basement, or if all else fails your classroom – to which jumble can be brought at the beginning of school each day. You will need to drive round to pick up the larger consignments whenever they are located by your team of pupils. And on the morning of the sale you will need to have a large party to sort out all the junk into various categories – men's, women's, children',s miscellaneous, shoes, nearly new, hardware, books, very miscellaneous, etc. When the sale itself begins, try to get a number of adults to supervise the stalls and act as 'store detectives' while your pupils man the individual stalls. You will need to have given them practice in the techniques of haggling and deciding on prices. At the end, try to get rid of everything, even if it means letting a dealer take it away for next to nothing: otherwise it will be hanging around your classroom for years to come.

Sponsored events used to be the stand-by of all fund-raising committees. But unless you are bright enough to come up with something really original, such events have probably been tried a few times too often in most schools. Many PTA's have for years relied for much of their income on the annual sponsored walk and sponsored swim: and as long as these are held during school time, and so involve missing lessons for the participants, they will always be popular with the children. However, most adults have long ago realized that sponsored events are merely a sweetened form of begging, and the present indications are that people are less and less ready to sponsor children, unless it is for some bizarre event that catches their sense of humour. Only you can decide in the context of your school whether a sponsored walk or swim or run or spell or silence or dance or sing or mental-arithmetic or ferret-trouser will have the effect of raising money or merely raising the public's exasperation.

I hope you will be able to dream up plenty more fund-raising ideas. Being in a school you have a vast human resource at your disposal, which gives you an immediate advantage over all the local charitable committees who are also trying to raise money. And once you have completed your first production, and it has with a bit of luck made a profit, you have a drama fund ready to place in the bank to subsidize your next production, and to use on capital expenditure – new lights, new dimmers, new rostrum blocks, proper flats – so that you can gradually build up a stock of drama and theatre equipment through the efforts of yourself and all the pupils involved in your productions.

12 The Performance

In the last few days leading up to the performance everything that you and your team have been working on must be drawn together. Since there is so much competition for the use of the school hall, it is likely to be only in the last few days that the set can be finally erected, the lighting rigged, and the seats put into place so that the hall starts to feel like a theatre. This is not a satisfactory arrangement: if you get the chance, it is much better to have the hall for at least a fortnight in advance, so that by the time of the first performance the actors are completely familiar with the set, the lights, the costumes, the props, and the whole feel of the theatrical situation.

But final rehearsals are inevitably fraught with frustrations. If you work hard at it, you may be able to persuade your head teacher to let you hold the dress rehearsal – possibly even some of the final technical run-throughs as well – during school time. This will solve your problems with children who would otherwise find it difficult to attend, and will positively delight the cast and backstage crew (which if you are not careful will swell considerably for these rehearsals); but it will incur the wrath of those of your colleagues who have to give up their free lessons to cover the classes of you and all the other teachers actively involved in the performance. My own attitude to this situation was to see this as the one chance for those teachers who had steadfastly had nothing to do with my production to make a contribution to its success – a chance I felt they ought to leap at with open arms. They seldom saw eye to eye with me on this issue. Whether you are able to adopt my attitude depends on how many of your colleagues are likely to support you, and how strong is the blessing of the Headmaster upon the enterprise. Teachers are perfectly within their rights to object to having to give up an hour of their free time to help the school play: the fact that you have given up hundreds of hours of your free time for the play will simply make you the more a fool in their eyes.

The dress rehearsal

The dress rehearsal must not be the first time that the actors have encountered any of the elements of the production. Each new element – costumes, lights, set, props – should be introduced separately, as early as possible, and not necessarily in the context of a full run-through or rehearsal. When the cast first try on their costumes, you will need a lengthy session to accustom them to moving and speaking in the costumes, to adjust those that do not fit, and to discuss what to do about dresses that looked superb on paper but may no longer suit the character as it has developed in rehearsal. And when the lights are first rigged you will need to devote a long time to adjusting them so as to eliminate unwanted shadows, to deciding what colour gels to insert in order to throw the right quality of light for each scene, and to going through the script to make every lighting change as slick as possible.

I have placed the dress rehearsal in a chapter entitled 'The Performance' because that is how it must be considered: as the first performance rather than as the last rehearsal. By this time all the work of directing the production is over: it is too late to add or change movements, to put extra polish on the actors' performances, to alter the lighting or redesign a costume. As director, you now take a seat in the audience and watch the performance through. The responsibility for the running of the show lies now with the stage manager.

In consultation with your stage manager, you must ensure that everything will go absolutely smoothly, and prepare for every possible eventuality. (Does everyone know the whereabouts of the first aid box and the fire extinguishers – and the broom for sweeping up broken light-bulbs?) The dress rehearsal is the time for ironing out any tiny last-minute hiccoughs in the production – undramatic pauses while a table is placed on stage; a scene-shifter wearing a shoe that squeaks; a wire that someone might trip over; a member of the chorus chattering just before their entry. Anything less trivial than this should have been dealt with long before. The aim of the dress rehearsal is to give everyone – actors and backstage crew alike – the experience of a complete performance under performance conditions.

Curtain calls

Some time in the final week you will need to devise and rehearse the curtain calls. The nature of these will depend on the style of your production. The simplest method is to bring all the cast on, let them bow once from the waist in unison, and let them leave the stage in an equally orderly fashion. At the other extreme, your curtain call could consist of a complex series of tableaux, with blackouts in between, featuring different sections of the cast and finally the whole cast. The traditional method of bringing on the lead characters one at a time in reverse order of importance seems to me to introduce a feeling of 'stars' which you have been struggling to avoid throughout the production – before you know where you are, your cast will be starting to compare the volume of applause received by each actor.

It is a shame for an unsuitable curtain call to break the atmosphere your play has created, so some sensitivity is needed to find a way of bringing the cast on to receive applause without spoiling the end of the play. In some circumstances – where, for example, a play has ended in a particularly tragic or thought-provoking way – it may be better not to have a curtain call at all: the audience will expect one, and to deny their expectation by leaving them with a bare stage may be the most appropriate ending for the play.

Confidence and morale

The one major responsibility that you retain through the dress rehearsal and the performances is for the confidence and morale of your cast. Stage nerves take different children in different ways: but they affect them all. If left to their own devices before a performance, some children will become silent and sluggish, others brittle and tearful, and yet others over-excited and rowdy. All will be tense (including you).

As I mentioned in Chapter Seven, the best way of controlling the various manifestations of stage nerves, unifying your cast, and focusing everyone's attention on the performance ahead, is to hold a warm-up session similar to those you have been holding at the start of all major rehearsals. Before a performance, the warm-up will probably need to be long and intense: the exercises strenuous and the relaxation period long, calm and uninterrupted.

Any speech-making you indulge in just before a performance must be gentle and general. If you give individual children specific finicky points just before they go on stage ('Don't forget to take an extra step downstage when you see Banquo's ghost') you may well confuse and worry them, and cause them to give a less convincing performance because they are busy thinking about stage technicalities rather than becoming their characters. What matters now is not where the actor stands during the banquet scene, but whether his terror at the appearance of the ghost is genuine. By the time the actors reach the stage all their thoughts should be in character, and any last-minute instructions you give them should either be in the form of generalized clichés designed to unify and enliven your acting team, or else consist of addressing the actors as their characters rather than as themselves.

Always have a supply of safety-pins backstage.

It is often said that a bad dress rehearsal means a good performance. It is not true; but there is a grain of truth there. A bad dress rehearsal will worry your cast, which might cause extra adrenalin to flow at the first performance, which might have a beneficial effect upon the amount of energy and concentration used by the performers; whereas a good dress rehearsal may lead to over-confidence which might cause silly mistakes and a lack of energy in the performance. You have to try to gauge the cast's feelings, and use the warm-up sessions before each show to strike a balance between under-confidence (leading to excessive and paralyzing fear on stage) and over-confidence (leading to a slipshod performance).

The middle performances are generally the most difficult in this respect. The first and last shows have an atmosphere of their own, simply because they are the first and last: all you have to do is to channel the actors' natural energy and excitement into the performance. In the middle performances the actors are likely to be very tired after the effort and tension of the first night, and they are likely to be over-confident and careless because they proved on the first night that they could give a good performance. So you may well need to make a special effort to get your actors alert, energized, and properly concentrating before they go on stage for these performances.

Prompters and understudies

I have never used a prompter in a play that I have directed, and I would strongly advise against it. If you have a prompter sitting by the stage, the actors will tend to use him: and use of a prompter completely destroys the illusion that the play is creating, breaking the rhythm of the scene and reminding actor and audience alike that the situation is one of children in a school hall rather than characters in a drama.

Provided that you have made sufficient use of improvisation in your rehearsals, that your actors have created characters that work, and that your cast is operating as a unified team, then they should be able to improvise their way out of any situation. If an expected character fails to enter, then those on stage should be able to invent additional dialogue to lead round to a repeat of the cue-line. If an actor 'dries' on stage, then those around him should be able to come straight in with leading questions that will steer him back to his correct lines. If the scenery collapses or a costume splits or the lights fuse, the actors should be capable of dealing with the situation without stepping out of character.

It will be worthwhile having some practice sessions at this a week or so before the performance. As an improvisation subject designed to help the actors to get into character, get them to deal with situations of forgotten lines, split clothing, and missed entries by improvising in character. Once the actors discover how easily this can be done, their general confidence will increase anyway, as they will realize that there is nothing that can go wrong which will seriously 'throw' them in performance.

The occasions when a prompter really is useful come during the middle period of the rehearsals, when the cast are rehearsing without scripts but are not yet fully sure of their lines. But it is easier to ask a member of the cast who is not on stage to prompt, rather than having a child specially brought in for this purpose. (In comic scenes, it is sometimes useful at this stage of rehearsals also to employ an 'interrupter' to howl with laughter from time to time so that the cast will not be surprised and disconcerted by audience laughter in the first performance.)

Some directors advocate a whole system of understudies, so that every actor is understudied by another actor who is taking a smaller part, or by a member of the chorus if there is one. Personally I have never done this: understudying involves all the huge effort of line-learning without the intensive rehearsal that makes this task easier, and probably without the satisfaction of performing the role in the end. It is a depressing task, calculated to discourage and put off even the most enthusiastic children.

It is very seldom that an actor in a major part will let you down. However ill a child is, such is the group loyalty that should have developed from your rehearsals that he will do his utmost to take part in the performances. In case of serious illness or injury, if you have a fortnight's notice or more, it may be possible to bring in another member of the cast to take over a role. But if a child suffers accident or illness any closer to the performance date, the best understudy is probably yourself or one of your colleagues involved in the production: someone who is already familiar with the script and so can learn the lines quickly, and above all someone who is an experienced actor and will not need to be taught how to act. If you have a pupil who fits the bill, and is not already playing a major role,then your problem will be solved. But otherwise the best answer is going to be an adult who has the confidence and stage experience to cope with the rapidly aproaching deadline of the first performance without undue panic. In other words, once again, probably yourself.

Front-of-house

With the press and the general public (you hope) coming into your school, it is necessary for you to give some thought to how the audience will be welcomed into the building, and how they will be looked after during the show and the interval.

Your front-of-house team have a wide range of responsibilities:

(a) checking that seats are neat, and there is no litter in the auditorium;

(b) selling tickets and programmes (and getting a cash float in advance for change);

(c) organizing car-parking;

(d) putting up direction signs to toilets and checking that toilets are clean;

(e) making and selling coffee at the interval (and washing up afterwards);

(f) checking that fire exits are not blocked;

(g) being aware, in consultation with the stage manager, of the procedure in case of fire or accident;

(h) making special arrangements for elderly or disabled members of the audience;

(i) making sure that there are not more tickets than seats;

(j) opening windows if the auditorium gets stuffy and closing them if it gets draughty;

(k) being polite to everyone;

(l) being utterly obsequious to press reporters, school governors, and the Headmaster.

Your front-of-house team can also take responsibility for the display of work in the foyer (ie the corridor leading to the hall or the classroom beside it). In Chapter Five I suggested some of the sorts of work that might be displayed here: sketches for scenery and posters from the art department; costume designs from the needlework department; the play's budget presented by the maths or commerce department; and project work relating to aspects of the play from the English, history, geography, craft, physics, and music departments, and any other departments you can justifiably drag in. The general impression you are trying to give is that every area of the school is involved in the play, and has contributed something. And thus the entire school, and not just a few actors, are responsible for the success of the play.

(For by now, at the end of Chapter Twelve, the performance is over: and it must have been a success!)

13 Conclusions

Has it all been worth it? On the next school morning after the last performance, you feel that your task is over, and you are ready to relax and recover from all the tension and exertion. But with gradually growing dismay you discover that there are still several weeks of term left; that your desk is covered with piles of exercise books that you haven't had time to mark during the week of the performances; and that for the majority of your colleagues and pupils nothing much has happened, and life goes on.

Then the aftermath of the play starts to grab at you. The head of PE sends a message asking if you can have all scenery cleared out of the hall in time for third lesson. The wardrobe mistress sends a message asking what happened to the expensive hired hat Lear's fool used in Act II. The Headmaster sends for you because one of the school governors thought she detected a socialist bias in the way you handled Act IV. And the actors all want to know when they can audition for the next production, and whether you can organize them a party to celebrate the success of the last one.

For a few days all this occupies you. You get the cast to organize their own party, and blearily supervise it, much in the way that you dealt with your fund-raising disco (see Chapter Eleven) except that the Headmaster probably lets you hold this event in school, and comes along to it himself in order to inhibit the festivities and make a speech congratulating everybody. You find out what became of everything hired and borrowed and gradually return it all to its owners. You clear all the scenery out of the hall – and as there is nowhere for it to be stored and it seems a shame to throw it away, it probably gets dumped in your classroom.

And then, gradually, you return to earth. The bright lights of the play are exchanged for the humdrum existence of a teacher; you rediscover just how demanding and exhausting teaching is, especially when you're feeling a bit down after all the tension and excitement of the last few weeks; and you wonder if you can ever face another production, how you survived the last one, and why you bothered.

If you have been totally successful, you have achieved a lot. You have unified all the disparate areas of your school in collaboration on a single project. You have given to all those actively involved the unforgettable group euphoria of a successful production. You have entertained the press, the public, the governors, the parents and the children, and have shown all of them how vital and exciting live theatre can be. You have contributed constructively to the adolescent development of your actors, giving them confidence, tolerance, sensitivity, and a unique experience of group activity. You have brought an artistic interest into the lives of children who had no previous experience of artistic endeavour, and who happily worked onstage or backstage with a devotion they have never before shown in any aspect of school life. You have promoted the good name of your school within the community surrounding it, and started to build up its reputation as a local cultural centre. You have shown even your most cynical colleagues that a school play need not be as bad a thing as they had supposed. You have made a profit. You, and all those involved, have had fun (well – retrospectively, anyway). You have built up in your colleagues and your pupils a strong and genuine enthusiasm for the arts in general and theatre in particular.

And if you have achieved only some parts of this: well, do not be too downhearted. We are learning all the time.

There is always your next production......

Appendix One
Jargon

(Useful for baffling or impressing your colleagues, and for understanding some of the books listed in Appendix Three).

Apron   Area of stage extending towards the audience from the proscenium arch.

ASM   Assistant stage manager – a euphemism for scene-shifter and dogsbody.

Aside   A line addressed to the audience or to certain characters, which other characters are not supposed to be able to hear.

Box set   Scenery which completely surrounds the actors on three sides, to give the effect of a room.

Corpsing   Uncontrollable nervous giggling on stage.

Curtain-call   The moment at the end of a show where the cast troop onto the stage and bow and you hope the audience will clap.

Cyclorama   Large white screen or wall behind the stage, onto which lighting effects can be projected.

Double-take   The staple gesture of most TV comedies, in which an actor at first looks at something without seeing it, and then after turning away realizes what he has seen.

Downstage   Towards the audience.

Dry   To forget one's lines on stage (usually accompanied by complete mental blank and panicked paralysis).

Flats   Pieces of scenery (see Chapter Nine).

Flies   Space above the stage, from which scenery can be 'flown' – ie winched up and down on ropes.

Gel   (Originally short for 'gelatine') a coloured filter placed in a socket in front of a light to change the colour of the beam.

Irony   The dramatic situation where some characters (and/or the

101

audience) are aware of something which other characters are not aware of.

Mask   To stand between the audience and another actor.

Mime   Acting without words or props.

Prompt Side   In some books Stage Left is referred to as PS and Stage Right as OPS. These letters stand for Prompt Side and Opposite Prompt Side, and are based on the assumptions that (a) your actors cannot tell their right hands from their left and (b) if you had a prompter he would be sitting on the left side of the stage. For further clarification or mystification see 'Stage Directions'.

Proscenium   A 'picture-frame' archway over the front of a stage.

Stage Left/Stage Right   Taken from the actors' point of view – ie Stage Right is the left side of the stage as far as the audience is concerned.

Stage Directions   Some dramatists try to baffle actors with a complex series of letters to denote different areas of the stage: eg UR = upstage right, DC = downstage centre. For further method of confusing actors see 'Prompt Side'.

Strike   To remove or dismantle (of scenery).

Subtext   What the characters are thinking, as opposed to what they are saying.

Throw-away   A line (usually comic) underplayed or delivered lightly, as if the character considers it unimportant.

Thrust Stage   A stage without proscenium arch, extending out into the audience.

Upstage   The part of the stage furthest away from the audience.

Upstage (verb transitive)   To stand upstage of another actor, so that in order to relate to you he has to turn his back on the audience, thus making you the focus of attention.

Wings   Area each side of the stage but hidden from the audience, where scene-shifters lurk and actors get in each others' way while waiting to enter.

For additional pretentiousness, many of these terms can be made more esoteric by abbreviating them – eg 'The pros arch is too close to the cyc to fit the floods in'. Keep this sort of line handy for when the Headmaster comes to watch a rehearsal.

Appendix Two
A twelve week schedule

(A rough guide to what needs to be done during the build-up to your production.)

Before the twelve weeks begin
Choose play. Read it and get to know it thoroughly. Apply for performance permission if necessary. Acquire copies of script. Produce rough budget. Get Head Teacher's approval for the whole project. Plan the practicalities of the production with stage manager, designer, costume designer, etc. Try to interest other teachers in using themes connected with the play in their syllabuses.

First week
Announce play to school. Hold preliminary auditions. Try to bully other teachers into being involved.

Second week
Final audition and casting. First rehearsals to familiarize cast with play. Finalize set design and see that work on set construction begins. Send letter to parents of children in cast.

Third week
Produce rehearsal schedule. Finalize costume designs and see that work on these is begun. Start quest for props. Check lighting equipment and arrange to acquire anything you will need.

Fourth week
In rehearsals, plot moves for one act at a time. Poster should be designed and printed by now. Check make-up stock and order anything you need. Produce final budget and arrange to raise money if ends won't meet otherwise.

Fifth week
In rehearsals, movements are now worked out for all scenes. Check that royalties have been paid.

Sixth week
Tickets should be designed and printed by now. In rehearsals, more detail on character.

Seventh week
All lines learnt by now. From here onwards, work on detail and interpretation in rehearsals. Also begin detailed coaching of individual actors.

Eighth week
All props complete and available for use in rehearsal from now on. Tickets on sale in school. First of weekly press releases sent to local paper. Information sent to 'What's On?' desks at local radio and television stations.

Ninth week
All costumes complete. All sound effects complete. Produce revised rehearsal schedule for final weeks. See that posters are displayed throughout the district. Tickets now on sale to general public. Send letter to all parents advertising the play. Start detailed preparation of foyer display.

Tenth week
Scenery now complete. Programmes designed and printed. First advertising gimmick in local town. Formal invitations with complimentary tickets sent to mayors, school governors, county officials, press, etc. Check first-aid and emergency procedures.

Eleventh week
Lighting is now complete. Excerpt from play shown in school assembly. All sale-or-return tickets now back at central box office. Final advertising gimmick in local towns. Final technical run-throughs. Photo session. Rehearse curtain calls. Buy coffee, milk, sugar, etc. for interval.

Twelfth week
Dress rehearsal. Foyer display erected. Check that enough seats are in auditorium. Check that car parks, toilets, etc, are clearly labelled and signposted. Review ready for local paper if they don't send a reporter. Performances. Sigh of relief.

(This schedule is designed to be a rough guide rather than a definitive set of rules. Obviously the timing of each aspect of your production will vary with the circumstances of your school and the nature of your play.)

104

Appendix Three
Books about theatre and drama

(A highly selective list of books you might find useful).

History of theatre

Hartnoll, Phyllis *A Concise History of the Theatre*
  Thames and Hudson – *lavishly illustrated*
Ward, Steve *The Theatre* Evans Bros. – a simpler book aimed at CSE
  level

Improvisation and teaching drama

Scher, Anna and Verrall, Charles *One Hundred Plus Ideas for Drama*
  Heinemann
Chilver, Peter *Teaching Improvised Drama* Batsford
Spolin, Viola *Improvisation for the Theater* Pitman
Clegg and Billing, Pemberton *Teaching Drama* ULP
Way, Brian *Development Through Drama* Longmans
Self, David *A Practical Guide to Drama in the Secondary School*
  Ward Lock
Brandes, Donna and Phillips, Howard *Gamester's Handbook*
  Hutchinson
Schools Council *Learning Through Drama* Heinemann
  – not a handbook but a consideration of the nature and
  educational value of drama
Goodridge, Janet *Drama in the Primary School* Heinemann
Whittam, Penny *Speech and Drama in the Infant School* Ward Lock

Directing and producing plays

Practical
Roose-Evans, James *Directing a Play* Studio Vista
Chilver, Peter *Producing a Play* Batsford
Counsell, John *Play Direction* David and Charles

Theoretical
Brook, Peter *The Empty Space* McGibbon and Kee

Humorous
Green, Michael*The Art of Coarse Acting* Arrow

Acting

Voice
Berry, Cecily *Voice and the Actor* Harrap

Movement
Laban, Rudolf *The Mastery of Movement*Macdonald and Evans
Hobbs, William *Techniques of the Stage Fight* Studio Vista
Colson, Greta *Drama Skills* Barrie and Jenkins

As a profession
Swift, Clive *The Job of Acting* Harrap
Billington, M *The Modern Actor* Hamish Hamilton

Theoretical
Stanislavsky *An Actor Prepares* Penguin

Theatre Crafts

Hoggett, Chris *Stage Craft* Black
Allensworth, Carl *The Complete Play Production Handbook*
    Robert Hale
Warre, Michael *Designing and Making Stage Scenery* Studio Vista
Motley *Theatre Props* Studio Vista
Kenton, Warren *Stage Properties and How to Make Them* Pitman
Bentham, Frederick *The Art of Stage Lighting* Pitman
Jackson, Sheila *Simple Stage Costumes and How to Make Them*
    Studio Vista
Cassin-Scott, Jack *Costumes and Settings for Historical Plays* Batsford
Peters, Joan and Sutcliffe Anna *Making Costumes for Plays* Batsford
Corson, Richard *Stage Make-up* Prentice-Hall
Perrottet, Philippe *Practical Stage Make-up* Studio Vista
Jones, Eric *Make-up for School Plays* Batsford
Snook, Barbara *Making Masks* Batsford

Other Useful Books

Kohler *A History of Costume* Dover
Palmer, Roy *A Touch on the Times* Penguin Education
(and many other excellent historical folk-song collections by the same author).

Appendix Four
Some plays suitable for production in schools

Full-length plays

The Frogs, Aristophanes (10 m 3 f + chorus): an ambitious choice, but offering exciting possibilities for an inventive and zany production if contemporary references are updated to deal with modern politicians, etc.

The Royal Hunt of the Sun Peter Shaffer (22 m 2 f + extras): famous modern play about the Spanish conquest of the Incas; needs two very strong leading actors, but offers possibilities for a spectacular staging in a boys' school.

Under Milk Wood Dylan Thomas (32 m 37 f): though written for radio, this play offers a good deal of scope for a stage production.

Mother Courage and Her Children Bertolt Brecht (18 m 6 f + extras): a play about the horror of war as seen by a canteen woman and her family in the Hundred Years War; needs a very strong lead actress, but offers a large number of good small parts and opportunities for interesting use of stylized movement, etc; contains a number of songs.

The Caucasian Chalk Circle Bertolt Brecht (28 m 12 f + extras): another excellent script for an ambitious school or theatre workshop group; many opportunities for interesting characterization, improvisation within the text, and large crowd scenes.

Tom Jones Joan Macalpine (16 m 9 f): although obviously it leaves out much of Fielding's novel, this adaptation captures the lively and bawdy atmosphere of the original; a highly entertaining play with lots of good characters.

The Insect Play The Brothers Kapek (cast: large): a fascinating and entertaining look at the world through the ways of life of various groups of insects – ants, butterflies, and dung beetles. A highly dramatic play with exciting possibilities for dance and costume.

Billy Liar Keith Waterhouse and Willis Hall (3 m 5 f): an entertaining play focusing on the problems of a boy at odds with the world in which he is growing up.

The Crucible Arthur Miller (11 m 11 f): an intense drama set in an American town which becomes obsessed with witch-hunting; a very ambitious choice for a school play, but very rewarding if you have the resources to do it.

The Apprentices, Peter Terson (cast: large): written for the National Youth Theatre; a play about young people at work in a factory.

Zigger Zagger, Peter Terson (cast: large): a loud and lively play that looks at problems of contemporary youth through the vigour of football mania; exciting possibilities for crowd work.

Ross, Terence Rattigan (22 m): a play about the life of Lawrence of Arabia; requires a very strong lead actor.

Chips with Everything, Arnold Wesker (19 m): another good modern play suitable for a boys' school, about the RAF.

The Kitchen, Arnold Wesker (18 m 12 f): set in the kitchen of a big London restaurant, this play looks at the horrifying pressures upon a group of people working together in inhuman conditions.

The Italian Straw Hat, Eugene Labiche (13 m 8 f + extras): a quick-moving farce with a wealth of entertaining characters.

Thieves Carnival, Anouilh (9 m 5 f): an entertaining spoof about a gang of professional thieves.

A Candle in the Dark, F. Roy Bennett (cast: large): a new play about Joan of Arc, written by a teacher from Yeovil for his own pupils; can be effectively staged in the round.

The Thwarting of Baron Bolligrew, Robert Bolt (cast: large): an amusing modern adventure fantasy, throwing traditional pantomime-type characters into a modern setting.

The Chicken Run, Aidan Chambers (11 m 6 f): a play about teenagers, involving newspaper rounds and motor-bike gangs.

Sweeney Todd, Austin Rosser (10 m 3 f): a classic Victorian melodrama with exciting possibilities for props and musical accompaniment.

The Adventures of Gervase Becket, Peter Terson (cast: large): a boisterous comedy about a country squire who volunteers to change places with anyone who is unhappy, and thereby encounters a series of adventures.

By Common Consent, Paul Thompson (cast: large): a political fantasy set in the future, in which the youth of the country have been mobilized as the keepers of law and order. A provocative play involving speech, mime, pageantry and music.

The Golden Masque of Agamemnon, John Wiles (cast: about 40): a masque, with speech, songs and movement, based on the Greek legends; written for the Cockpit Youth Summer Workshop.

The Children's Crusade, Paul Thompson (cast: large): an historical play about the ill-fated crusade; opportunities for movement and crowd work and music.

The Dream of Chief Crazy Horse, David Pownell (cast: large): an epic pageant play spanning 10,000 years in the history of the Red Indian; written for a secondary school production.

Kes, Alan Stronach (20 m 5 f): a skilful adaptation of the novel; the hawk is the leading character but never appears on stage.

The Roses of Eyam, Don Taylor (cast: large): a powerful piece of theatre suitable for an ambitious group; has been performed by Taunton Youth Theatre, and seen on television.

Brunel, Keith Parker (cast: large): the life and achievements of the great Victorian engineer shown in a series of rumbustious scenes.

The Wellesbourne Tree, Robert Leach (18 m 9 f + extras): a documentary drama about Joseph Arch and the founding of the National Agricultural Labourers Union; the play includes folk songs collected by Roy Palmer.

The Doctor and the Devils, Dylan Thomas (cast: large): a film scenario that can be effectively adapted for the stage, telling the story of Burke and Hare.

Musicals

West Side Story, Bernstein, Sondheim and Laurents (22 m 12 f + choruses): needs highly competent musical director and choreographer, and two good singers for Tony and Maria; a highly exciting and moving show which children can really identify with.

Grease, Jim Jacobs and Warren Casey (9 m 8 f + chorus): a highly entertaining '50s Rock'n'Roll musical with songs and dances that will greatly appeal to children of secondary school age; unlike the film, the stage show has an even spread between the ten main characters; the text may need bowdlerizing a little for some schools,

110

and the story is fairly slender, but it will appeal to children because it concerns the problems of schoolchildren.

Girl Crazy, George and Ira Gershwin (cast: large): a send-up of the Wild West, with some well-known Gershwin songs and opportunities for spectacular dance routines.

The Beggar's Opera, John Gay (14 m 12 f + extras): the famous eighteenth century ballad opera still wears well if handled with gusto.

The Threepenny Opera, Brecht and Weill (7 m 4 f + extras): Brecht's updated version of Gay's original contains many opportunities for stage movement as well as Weill's splendidly abrasive songs.

Oh What a Lovely War, Theatre Workshop with Charles Chilton (12 m 3 f + chorus): lively anti-war show about the First World War, using contemporary soldiers' songs.

Oliver, Lionel Bart (cast: large): the famous musical version of *Oliver Twist* must have been done in just about every school in the country by now.

Joseph and the Amazing Technicolour Dreamcoat, Tim Rice and Andrew Lloyd-Webber (cast: large): the music for this show has also found its way into just about every school in the country; it can make a spectacular and entertaining stage show, although you may not be able to get permission to stage it if it is still being done professionally.

Short Plays

The Mock Doctor, Henry Fielding (8 m 3 f): an entertaining translation of Moliere's *Le Médecin Malgrè Lui* with some amusing characters and opportunities for further updating.

Wish You Were Here, Norman Smithson and Alfred Bradley (6 m 5 f): a family on the beach, and everything that goes wrong as they desperately try to enjoy themselves; opportunities for a number of extras to build up the beach atmosphere.

He Who Says Yes/He Who Says No, Bertolt Brecht: two related scripts that lend themselves for experimental work with possible use of stylized movement, choral speaking, masks, music, mime.

A Villa On Venus, Kenneth Lillington (cast: 10): a space romp involving intrepid astronauts, bug-eyed monsters, and endless opportunities for visual comedy and extras.

111

The Youth Club, Patrick Murray (18 m 8 f + extras): a play written by a teenager about teenagers, dealing with the closure of a youth club.

The Incredible Vanishing, Denise Coffey (cast: 10): a barrow-boy, a meter maid and a policeman find themselves in the under-street world of the goblins; opportunity for improvisation and audience participation.

Adam's Ark, Harold Hodgson (13 m 8 f): a disturbing look at the future, with a party of children and their teacher experiencing a Nuclear War; some good opportunities for characterization, humour and excitement.

The Coming of the Kings, Ted Hughes (cast: large): a modern nativity combining humour and comic business with the simplicity and tenderness of the Christmas story.

Carrigan Street, John Pick (cast: large): a lively play about a community's efforts to prevent a street being demolished to make way for a ring road.

The Mask of Anubis, G. Thomas (cast: large): a murder play with opportunities for movement, dance and singing, and the use of masks and spectacular costumes; written for a group of children studying ancient Egypt.

Hutchinson publish a number of excellent anthologies of short plays suitable for use in secondary schools:

Playbill One, Playbill Two, Playbill Three, Second Playbill One, Second Playbill Two, Second Playbill Three, Prompt One, Prompt Two, Prompt Three, all edited by Alan Durband; and *Act One, Act Two, Act Three*, edited by David Self and Ray Speakman. The following plays can be found in these books.

Ernie's Incredible Illucinations, Alan Aykbourn (cast: large): a delightful comedy about a boy whose daydreams become reality; great opportunity for crowd work, *(Playbill One)*.

Arthur, David Cregan (cast: large): a fantasy about a boy's reluctant rebellion against the older generation; many good comic roles plus three comic choruses – firemen, policewomen and boy scouts. *(Playbill One)*.

The Crickets Sing, Beverly Cross (8 m 3 f + extras): a play set in the English Civil War, with much comic potential and opportunity for period costumes *(Playbill One)*.

School Play, Donald Howarth (cast: variable): an experimental play about a class reading a play with menacing overtones as it develops *(Playbill One)*.

The Rising Generation, Ann Jellicoe (cast: large): a fascinating fantasy set in a world dominated by women, where men are outlawed, hunted, killed, and sold as slaves; much opportunity for experimental acting and crowd work *(Playbill Two)*.

Excursion, Alan Plater (7 m 7 f): a selection of people take the train to town for a day out; originally a radio play, but could be effectively staged with plenty of extras to build up the picture of the town on the day of the big match *(Playbill Three)*.

Burn-Up, Derek Bowskill (12 voices): a play needing an experimental approach to rhythms and vocal music, examining the age of living-for-kicks *(Second Playbill Two)*.

Weevils in my Biscuit, Charles Savage (8 m 4 f): another play for voices, a light-hearted naval revue based on authentic documentation *(Second Playbill Two)*.

Apples, C P Taylor (cast: 18): an allegory about a bunch of school leavers sent out by their teacher in search of symbolic apple trees *(Prompt One)*.

Island, Michael Barwis (cast: large): a fantasy about three children who try to cross the High Street and get stranded on a traffic island, where they are menaced by juggernauts; the attempts of the army, the police and the fire brigade to rescue them are in vain, and it is only when the whole world runs out of petrol that the children can escape *(Prompt One)*.

A Day in the Mind of Tich Oldfield, A England (10 m 3 f + extras): an imaginative romp based on the adventures of a boy with a fertile imagination.

Our Day Out, Willy Russell (cast: large): a bunch of kids on a school outing; recently made into a highly successful television film *(Act One)*.

Mr Bruin Who Once Drove The Bus, Donald Howarth (cast: large): another play set in a school, about the kindly but misunderstood driver of the school bus *(Act One)*.

Love Is A Many-Splendoured Thing, Alan Bleasdale (2 m 3 f + extras): a touching and funny play about two children sent to do a project about love *(Act One)*.

Family Ties, Peter Terson (8 m 9 f): a double bill consisting of two plays: *Never Right, Yet Again* and *Wrong First Time (Act Two)*.

In addition to all these, the Macmillan *Dramascript* series and the Dobson *Theatre in Education* series both contain much excellent material (full-length and shorter) specially prepared for use in schools.

Index